food for a happy gut

food for a happy gut

RECIPES TO CALM, NOURISH & HEAL

**NAOMI
DEVLIN**

HEADLINE

CONTENTS

HOW TO HAVE A HAPPY GUT

Pretty much every morning I wake up, clap my hands and wonder what I might eat for breakfast. I am a foodie, in love with the changing seasons that bring rhubarb in February, asparagus in May and plums in August, and I'm endlessly fascinated by the diverse flavours of food from around the world. I am not a trained chef and yet I have always cooked, devouring recipe books greedily as soon as I could read. From my teenage years in a rural commune, where I learnt to make great pots of spicy dal and bake show-stopping birthday cakes, to more recent holidays in Italy where the vegetables were so good they only needed a slick of olive oil to sing, cooking and eating have been at the centre of my life.

Food took on a different meaning for me for a while when I was diagnosed with coeliac disease, becoming a source of anxiety and often disappointment; restaurants were fraught with danger, and old favourites, like crusty bread, were off the menu. I could have sulked and pined for what I was missing, but I chose instead to embrace the new challenge and celebrate the wonderful things that I could still safely and joyfully eat. I learnt about the mysterious business of what goes on in the gut, and that what I ate, how I lived and my emotional state all had a profound influence on my health.

Eating is such an integral part of our lives and an opportunity for each of us to comfort, delight and nourish, that I have made it my mission to help others discover how delicious it can be to take care of your gut. These recipes encourage everyone to diversify their diet, including those who have no digestive issues but want to improve their microbiome and support their immune system, thus enjoying greater energy and wellbeing.

This book offers you over a hundred opportunities to expand your repertoire and feed your microbes interesting foods that allow them to flourish. Variety truly is the spice of life where your gut is concerned, so embrace your desire to try new things, knowing that this will make you more vital.

The key to eating well while leading our busy lives is to take a little time out each week to prepare food in advance. Soak and cook grains and pulses, slow cook some hard-working cuts of meat, make Bone Broth (see page 53), and get the family involved in some simple kitchen work to make a busy week fly by in a stream of delicious suppers.

Everything in this book is bursting with flavour and nothing is difficult to prepare; from Broad Bean Hummus (see page 120) to Lick-Your-Fingers Chicken (see page 86), a few choice ingredients can make any meal sing with flavour. By using wonderful fresh produce and filling your larder with pickles, sprinkles and sauces from the Heal section, your meals will reward you throughout the year, keeping both your taste buds and microbes interested. Try making a jar of spicy Dukkah (see page 218) or some Sunshine Sauerkraut (see page 202) to add instant zing to the simplest of plates.

I also encourage you to listen to the murmuring of your body as it guides you to what it needs. During busy times, it might tell you that it is really craving restorative Miso Soup (see page 57) and soothing Jelly Sweets (see page 100), or after an exhilarating run it would really like a refreshing glass of Water Kefir (see page 239). When your body gets the nourishment it craves, you will feel properly satisfied by your food, and when your microbes are happy, they will help you thrive in what promises to be a wonderful lifelong partnership. It doesn't matter who you are, absolutely everyone can benefit from giving their gut a little TLC.

HOW TO USE THIS BOOK

The three sections of the book, Calm, Nourish and Heal, represent a progression from meals that soothe and restore a troubled gut, to the inclusion of more challenging foods that really improve resilience and microbial diversity. No need to cook special meals for different family members, because everybody can benefit from the recipes whether their gut needs extra care or not.

CALM

The Calm section contains recipes that are low in FODMAPs (see page 12) and high in gut-soothing ingredients, such as Bone Broth (see page 53), omega-3 fats, probiotics and anti-inflammatories. This is the place to start if you have sensitive digestion or a stressful life that affects your gut. If you have coeliac disease or Irritable Bowel Syndrome (IBS), this section allows you to calm the inflammation that causes discomfort before you begin to feed up your microbes.

You may find that you need to adapt the recipes if you are following one of the other therapeutic diets (see Acid Reflux on page 12, IBS on page 12, Leaky Gut Syndrome on page 13, and Raised Histamine on page 14), or if you know that you have an intolerance to something specific. Wherever possible I have given alternatives, but you will know what suits you best.

As your gut heals and symptoms recede, start introducing the more advanced foods suggested in this section, for example, more onion, a little garlic, dandelion greens or broccoli, before moving on to try the less challenging recipes in the Nourish section. Start with moong dal (see Soothing Dal, page 180) when introducing pulses, and try the Coconut and Cauliflower Soup with Mussels (see page 132), or a recipe featuring cabbage when introducing brassicas. If you are unsure, try a half portion and serve it with something you know you can digest with ease. As you introduce new foods, your gut will get used to them in time.

NOURISH

Prebiotic food is the stuff that feeds the friendly bacteria in your gut. The Nourish section is full of prebiotic treats that will supply your microbes with an array of new things to munch. Although sometimes this might mean you are a little windy later in the day, this tends to decrease as your microbes find a contented and harmonious balance. If your digestion is untroubled, then these recipes are a great addition to your diet and can be made more diverse by, for example, changing the beans you use or adding a seasonal ingredient that arrived in the veg box that morning.

The recipes in this section also include probiotic fermented vegetables, anti-inflammatories and nourishing broths, but you can go heavy on the garlic, shave raw Jerusalem artichoke over your plate and feature brassicas in every meal, if your heart desires. Your reward will be increased vitality, resistance to infection and no trouble from passing vampires.

HEAL

The Heal section features all the crunchy, spicy, pickled bits that make life a little more interesting, and happily have a therapeutic value, too. From probiotic pickled vegetables and water kefir, to anti-inflammatory dressings, and sprinkles or bitters that tone your liver and stimulate digestive enzymes, everything here will enhance your meals, make your mouth water and get your digestive system ready for work.

If you are eating from the Calm section of the book, then make pickles with low FODMAP vegetables, such as Ribbon Pickle (see page 209), Probiotic Ketchup (see page 228) and Pickled Baby Courgettes (see page 201), plus some Water Kefir (see page 239) and a jar of digestive bitters (see page 246). Wherever possible, I have suggested ways to make the recipes in the Heal section more or less challenging for your digestion, according to what is suitable for you.

These are mostly recipes to make on a lazy Sunday and stock the pantry, so that the simplest of meals can be brought to life with a spoonful of this and a sprinkle of that. If you keep a jar of Kimchi (see page 198) and some leafy greens in the fridge, plus some cooked rice and beans in the freezer, then you'll soon be sitting down to a delicious gut-friendly meal that will keep you satisfied all evening.

GLUTEN-FREE INGREDIENTS

All of the recipes in this book are either inherently gluten free, or can easily be made so. That is not to say there is anything wrong with gluten, far from it, but if you need to eat gluten free, you can easily tailor the book to your own needs.

The key to good health is a diverse diet, so if you can tolerate gluten, choose from a variety of flours and don't just stick to the same bag of wheat flour, because you may find that you love the flavour of buckwheat or teff and have a soft spot for black rice noodles, just as I do.

Of the ingredients in the book, if you do need to follow a gluten-free diet, make sure you pay attention to the following and check that what you choose is safe for you to use: Worcestershire sauce, tamari, miso, baking powder, mustard (mustard powder may contain wheat, but Dijon, whole grain and pure mustard powder should be ok), ground spices, flours (choose the gluten-free options in the book; note that rye and spelt contain gluten), noodles (shirataki, rice and buckwheat are fine).

Where I have suggested sourdough bread, either make your own gluten-free sourdough if you cannot buy it easily (find recipes in my book, *River Cottage Gluten Free*), make Teff and Sesame Pancakes (see page 122), or use gluten-free oatcakes, if appropriate. I urge you not to eat the commercial gluten-free breads that contain lots of starch and emulsifiers, as these are likely to undermine some of the benefits of the recipes.

INTRODUCTION

DIGESTION FROM TOP TO BOTTOM

Digestion starts in the mouth as we chew our food and mix it with enzyme-rich saliva, which begins the long process of breaking it down into small molecules that can be absorbed in the small intestine. Feeling hungry, making supper and contentedly chewing your way through it, also helps your body get in the mood for digestion.

After your food has been chewed, it travels down the oesophagus (1) to the stomach. Food is slapped against the sides of the stomach (2) walls for a couple of hours and mixed with a potent solution of gastric juices (hydrochloric acid, salts and pepsin) that puts most harmful bacteria out of action and starts to unfold proteins, making them easier to break down.

Once the stomach is done squishing, the pulpy mixture moves to the small intestine (6), where the liver (3), gall bladder (4) and pancreas (5) deliver bile and digestive enzymes to help break down food into even smaller parts. This is where we absorb most of the nutrients from the food we eat. Anything not broken down becomes food for microbes that live in the large intestine (8). The small intestine twists and turns through the abdominal cavity for many metres; it is lined with velvety mucous tissue and tiny finger-like projections called villi that extend the surface area available to absorb nutrients.

Food spends an average of 3 hours winding its way through this part of the gut, after which the small intestine likes to tidy up, so the villi sweep any remaining particles along until everything is pristine again. The small intestine contains relatively few bacteria and needs to clean up regularly to stay that way, so if you constantly snack through the day and there's no time to clean up afterwards, bacteria can move in to squat where they are not wanted.

Now that most of the nutrients have been extracted, the remaining fibre, soluble carbohydrates and other indigestible bits move onto the relative calm of the large intestine, a very different place from the velvety, bustling small intestine. At the junction where the two meet is the appendix (7), made of the same immune tissue as your tonsils, which acts as nightclub bouncer for the large intestine by detecting any rogue bacteria trying to sneak past. If it senses anything untoward, the appendix marshals the immune system to mount an attack and the intruders are despatched. Although harmful bacteria can sometimes cause the appendix to overreact, leading to a bout of appendicitis, it is also a repository for many of the beneficial bacteria that make up our gut flora, enabling us to repopulate after gastroenteritis or a course of antibiotics has wiped out many of the good guys.

Past the appendix and into the horseshoe-shaped large intestine, with walls rich with immune cells, everything slows down to a stately pace and the parts of our food that cannot be broken down and absorbed in the small intestine become food for the millions of bacteria that live there. These bacteria feed us back by breaking down soluble fibre and indigestible carbohydrate to produce many beneficial substances, such as anti-inflammatory fatty acids, B vitamins and vitamin K. They also help us to regulate blood cholesterol and excrete hormones and waste products from metabolism. Food spends about 16 hours on this last part of its journey, as the bacteria need lots of time to work. The rectum (9) is the last stop on the long journey through the digestive system.

We don't tend to talk very much about what goes on in any part of our gut, but especially not about what happens at the very end. Yet it can be an excellent indicator of good or poor gut health. For information on whether your poo is healthy or not, I refer you to the Bristol Stool Chart which you can find online.

WHEN THINGS GO WRONG IN YOUR GUT

The bacteria that live on both the inside and outside of your body are called your microbiome. They are as unique to each of us as our fingerprints and are influenced by all sorts of things, good and bad. A period of intense stress might have a negative effect on your gut, while a sunny summer spent eating lots of fresh veg and working outside can have a positive effect. This effect is not just because anxiety may cause your muscles to tense; your emotions can actually change the behaviour of your microbes in your gut. Everything you eat, inhale, touch and feel has the potential to influence your microbiome. When harmful bacteria outnumber the beneficial bacteria this is called dysbiosis.

The things that could cause dysbiosis are: eating processed food, damaged fats, too much meat or sugar, drinking too much alcohol, taking medications (especially antibiotics, oral contraceptives, antacids and proton pump inhibitors) and using anti-bacterial products. By starving beneficial microbes of the food and environment they need to thrive, we allow harmful bacteria to take their place.

ACID REFLUX AND THE GORD DIET

Your stomach is full of acid that is corked in place by a valve called the oesophageal sphincter that opens just long enough to accept a bit of food and then shuts quickly. Although we all swallow many times a day without a thought, the nerves that govern the junction between the oesophagus and stomach are performing acrobatic feats each time we do so and sometimes they misfire, allowing acid to leak upwards and cause heartburn or reflux (GORD). This can be exacerbated by a period of stress, dysbiosis and certain foods that cause the oesophageal sphincter to relax and leak acid. Although antacids and proton pump inhibitors will help in the short term, long term, you need that acid to break down food and inhibit harmful bacteria and viruses.

The plan: to heal GORD you must temporarily remove everything that relaxes the oesophageal sphincter while improving your gut flora. Look for a good probiotic supplement containing *Lactobacillus plantarum* and bifidobacteria, such as *Bifidobacterium infantis*, *B. longum* or *B. breve*, but avoid those with a high FOS (fructo oligosaccharide) content as this can cause bloating. Healing broths and anti-inflammatory fats will help to restore the integrity of the digestive tract. Follow the diet below for 4–5 weeks and then start to include restricted foods, one at a time, to see if they are problematic, but continue to nourish your gut and take probiotics for 3 months. Finding ways to de-stress will help you avoid those misfiring oesophageal nerves. Eat from the Calm section of the book until you feel better.

Avoid the following for about a month: fruit, milk, cream, spices, sugar, alcohol, honey, maple syrup, agave syrup, tomatoes, cocoa, coffee, garlic, mint.

Healing broth: make or buy meat or fish Bone Broth (see page 53) and drink a small glass of this with each meal to encourage your digestive juices, or make soup, if you prefer. Vegetarians can make vegetable stock with a 10cm (4in) piece of kombu added to it after it has been taken off the heat, but this is not nearly as effective as animal-based broths.

IBS, BLOATING AND FODMAPS

If you have IBS (Irritable Bowel Syndrome), you will be familiar with the painful abdominal bloating, cramps and unpredictable bowel habits that characterise this condition. The small intestine is often irritated in IBS sufferers and many struggle to break down certain carbohydrates. This is particularly the case if you have dysbiosis, because harmful bacteria may cause inflammation. While diet can help with the symptoms of IBS, stress relief is an important part of managing the condition.

The plan: FODMAP is the acronym for Fermentable Oligosaccharides, Disaccharides, Monosaccharides and Polyols – complex sugars to you and me. Foods that contain these sugars could also be referred to as flatulent foods, because they are notorious for causing wind in those who can't break them down, so some people must follow a low FODMAP diet to manage their symptoms. Some people are more sensitive to fructose, while others have issues with one of the other saccharides or with polyols, so the range of problem foods will vary. The low FODMAP diet is only a temporary measure to adopt while you heal your gut, otherwise beneficial microbes will start to suffer from the lack of food that they like. Eat from the Calm section of the book until you feel better.

Below is a list of foods that contain significant quantities of FODMAPs. Rather than treating this like an allergy list of foods to avoid, you may find that small amounts or one or two of them are fine, but a meal composed entirely of these foods leaves you in pain. Foods in *italics* are best avoided if you are sensitive, and everything else be cautious with.

Vegetables: asparagus, artichoke (globe and *Jerusalem*), beetroot, broad bean, cabbage, cauliflower, celery, dandelion greens, *garlic*, kale, leek (except green parts), mangetout, *onion* (except the green part of spring onions), pulses, salsify.

Fruit: apple, apricot, avocado, blackberry, blackcurrant, cherry, date, fig, grapefruit, lychee, mango, nectarine, peach, pear, plum, pomegranate, prune, raisin, watermelon.

Grains: amaranth, barley, farro, kamut, rye, spelt, triticale, *wheat*.

Nuts: almond (small quantities are ok), cashew, peanut, pistachio.

Dairy: cream, milk, soft cheese, yoghurt (may be ok in small quantities).

When you start reintroducing FODMAPs, do so slowly, gradually increasing the quantity you eat of problem foods, but focusing on diversity rather than eating large quantities of any one thing. If you start to experience symptoms again, reduce your intake and focus on gut healing a little longer.

Digestive enzymes: in order to help break down FODMAPs more effectively, it can be helpful to take a digestive enzyme (available from health food shops). Take one with each meal for a month or so and then stop for a week and assess whether you want to continue. When you start adding in more challenging foods, you may want to start taking them again, but your pancreas and liver should start to get the message after a little while and ramp up production of natural enzymes and bile.

FOOD INTOLERANCE AND LEAKY GUT SYNDROME

As food is broken down into its constituent parts on its journey through the small intestine, the cells of the mucosa part imperceptibly to allow particles access to the blood stream. Some foods (especially those containing gluten or plant lectins) cause the cells to stay open a little longer and may allow larger, unbroken down particles to enter the blood stream. This is called having a leaky gut or intestinal permeability and can be exacerbated by: certain antibiotics, some medications (including oral contraceptives), food additives (particularly emulsifiers), alcohol, emotional stress, and bacteria which have no business being in the small intestine.

The most common symptoms are food intolerance, seasonal allergies, joint pain, chronic fatigue, inflamed sinuses, hives, rashes, rosacea and IBS.

The plan: to heal a leaky gut, you need to deal with the reasons that your gut is more permeable, and also repair the gut lining. Slow-cooked cuts of meat on the bone and any fish cooked on the bone will help, as will a regular intake of meals containing Bone Broth (see page 53), because amino acids contained in the connective tissue can soothe the gut lining and aid cell repair. You may also take powdered (hydrolysed) collagen as a supplement, added to soups, smoothies and porridges at a rate of 2–4 heaped tablespoons per day.

Lecithin is also good to include in your diet, initially in the form of egg yolks, oily fish, meat, tofu and leafy vegetables, and later add in brassicas, tempeh and pulses as your digestion improves. Try the Calm section of the book first.

Avoid: for the first month, avoid gluten-containing grains, alcohol, caffeine, unfermented dairy, sugar, refined foods and emulsifiers, such as carrageenan. Be cautious with FODMAPs (see page 12) and raw food during this time and, wherever possible, limit your intake of medication, although you should always discuss this with your prescriber.

RAISED HISTAMINE AND HISTAMINE INTOLERANCE

Mast cells in our tissues release histamine in response to foreign proteins, allowing white blood cells greater access to fight off the invader. We then produce an enzyme (diamine oxidase) to deactivate any circulating histamine that is no longer needed, but some people do not produce as much of this enzyme and some foods block it too, leading to raised histamine levels and chronic problems like sinusitis, itching, hives, tinnitus, headaches, loose stools or constipation, low blood pressure, irregular heart beat and dizziness. Histamine is also produced and degraded by different bacteria in the gut, so your microbiome can influence histamine levels, too. Some of the foods you eat every day also contain histamine, and others release stored histamine into your tissues, causing a bout of itching, sneezing or flushing. By reducing foods that contain histamine and histamine releasers, symptoms are reduced.

The plan: for a couple of weeks, completely eliminate foods containing significant amounts of histamine, histamine releasers and diamine oxidase blockers, and then relax a little bit, until you find the level that you can tolerate. Follow the diet below for at least 3 months and then you should be able to include more foods that contain histamine.

High histamine foods: alcohol, aged meat, cured meat, all fish and shellfish (especially tinned or cured), hard cheese, fermented food, vinegar and pickled food, walnut, cashew, peanut, soya bean, tempeh, chickpea, cocoa powder and chocolate.

Histamine releasers: citrus fruit (lemon and lime are ok), kiwi, pineapple, plum, strawberry, avocado, papaya, tomato, nuts, cocoa powder and chocolate, wheat germ, beans, pulses, food additives (such as sulphites, sulphur dioxide and nitrites).

Diamine oxidase blockers: alcohol, black and green tea, rooibos tea, mate tea.

Supplements and medicine foods: there are several supplements and some foods that you can add to your diet to reduce your histamine levels naturally:

• **Quercetin** is a naturally occurring flavonoid that can reduce histamine levels. You can take a supplement or include the following foods in your diet: caper (salted), lovage, sorrel, radish top, carob, dill, coriander leaf, red pepper, fennel top, red onion, radicchio, watercress, buckwheat, kale, apple.
• **Vitamin C** is known to reduce histamine, so try these foods and food-based supplements (in descending order of potency), many of which can be bought powdered to add to food: acerola berry, sea buckthorn, Indian gooseberry, rosehip, blackcurrant, red pepper, parsley, broccoli, redcurrant, goji berry.

- **The Lactobacillus strains**, *Lactobacillus plantarum, L. salivarius, L. rhamnosus, Bifidobacterium infantis* and *B. longum* are known to reduce histamine levels. Avoid supplements containing *Lactobacillus casei, L. delbrueckii* and *L. bulgaricus*, and be cautious with yoghurts that list these in the culture.
- **Your gut lining** is where the histamine-reducing enzymes are formed, so support this with bone broths and head to the Heal section of the book for bitters and teas to soothe and support your liver.

PROBIOTICS

Probiotic is the term used for any food, drink or supplement that contains beneficial bacteria. Can you believe that we carry more than ten times as many bacterial cells on our skin and in our gut than we have human cells in the rest of our body? We are, in fact, more genetically bacterial than anything else, and these microbial communities who live on and in us are called our microbiome. Our gut flora, or more correctly, gut microbiota, act like an extra organ because they perform so many metabolic duties for us, metabolising substances that we can't break down ourselves and fermenting undigested carbohydrates to produce beneficial fatty acids, vitamin K and B complex vitamins. They help us to excrete unwanted cholesterol and maintain a good blood lipid balance. By interacting positively with our immune system, bacteria can even help us produce happy hormones and influence our mood.

Rather than focusing on specific types of microbes being more beneficial than others, the current wisdom is that diversity of species is the most important factor in health. Microbes will colonise our gut according to where and how we live and what food we give them, not just which supplements we take, so it is important to try and get your microbes from a wide variety of sources and not just out of a bottle.

Not all bacteria are beneficial and some can be very harmful indeed in large numbers (*MRSA, E. coli* and *Salmonella* for example) and many people now get rid of all the bacteria in their homes by using antibacterial products. However small amounts of harmful bacteria have been shown in studies to prime the immune system and keep it fighting fit, reducing overreactions like anaphylaxis. These micro-exposures happen when we garden or stroke a dog, for example. It is still very important to take sensible precautions to prevent food spoiling and take care not to spread infection, but you do not need to sanitise everything.

SOURCES OF PROBIOTICS

Fermented vegetables and beans: lacto fermented vegetables, such as sauerkraut and kimchi, and fermented bean dishes, such as miso, tempeh and natto, are enjoyed for their sour, savoury, umami flavours and probiotic benefits. Fermenting breaks down some of the fibre into a form that is less likely to induce wind and allows beneficial bacteria to grow, transforming humble beans and vegetables into superfoods with more available nutrients and enhanced vitamin content. They are saltier than ordinary foods, and eaten more as a relish or pickle. Those who suffer from high histamine levels should be cautious about adding fermented food to their diets. See Raised Histamine (page 14).

SCOBYs: an acronym for Symbiotic Communities of Bacteria and Yeast, used to describe cultures for fermenting milk or sugar water or grains into kefir, kombucha and sourdough.

Cultured dairy: fermented dairy contains lots of beneficial bacteria and sometimes fungi or yeasts that contribute to the diversity of the microbiome. Raw (unpasteurised) dairy products contain beneficial enzymes and probiotics that are damaged during pasteurisation. Avoid raw dairy products if you have immunodeficiency (during chemotherapy for example), are pregnant or for children under three.

Preserved meat: dry-cured salami and ham use controlled fermentation to preserve the meat, creating probiotic delicacies when made without the use of lactose, dextrose and various preservatives. Look for products that contain just meat, fat, salt, garlic or spices.

Animals: owning a pet (especially a dog) and living or working on a farm are associated with greater diversity of gut bacteria. Although we don't yet know why, it does appear that this diversity helps to support immune function, damp down allergies and reduce food intolerance. If you don't have your own animals, try to say hello to any that you meet if it seems appropriate. You don't have to kiss them to take some of the bacteria home with you. The exception to this is cat litter trays, as cats carry toxoplasmas that are not beneficial. Always wash your hands thoroughly after changing a litter tray and avoid completely if pregnant or immunocompromised.

Gardening: the soil contains bacteria and fungi that we just don't have in our diets any more due to the sanitisation of everything from vegetables to water. Even if you don't have a garden, you can get your hands dirty and grow something in a window box, allotment or community gardening scheme. Other benefits are improved vitamin D levels from exposure to sunlight, and breathing more deeply as you focus on some mentally undemanding work.

Eating with your hands: you may have been told off for eating with your hands once you graduated from the high chair, but it can be a wonderful way to connect with your food and get a little micro-exposure to some dirt. I'm not suggesting that you don't wash your hands first – just make sure that you do it only with soap and water and nothing anti-bacterial. If you have been gardening, maybe just rinse off the dirt and sit on

the grass to eat. When you eat with your hands, you can become more aware of food as a sensual pleasure and are less likely to wolf down your meal.

PREBIOTICS AND FIBRE

Prebiotics are the foods that our gut bacteria like to munch on. It is important that you give your microbial passengers the sort of meals they like, as they will keep you healthy and happy in return. So try to include as many foods as you can tolerate from the lists below – remember that variety is super important here.

Insoluble plant fibre: the tough stuff that gives plants their structure can't be digested, but travels through the digestive system, giving bulk to your poo and helping the gut to move faster. As it makes its way through the gut, it takes dead cells, hormonal by-products, heavy metals and toxins with it, easing the eliminative burden on the organs. Found in chewy foods like whole grains, pulses, vegetables (especially their skins), nuts, seeds and fruit (especially berries).

Soluble plant fibre: inulin, pectin, beta-glucans and oligosaccharides represent some of the fibres that dissolve in water to make a gelatinous substance that slows the transit of food through the gut, soothes inflammation and is fermented by the gut microbiota. Aim to eat a wide variety of soluble fibre rather than taking supplements.

Be aware that some of this fibre can cause a lot of fermentation, so start gently if you aren't used to eating it. Good sources are: whole grains (especially wheat, oats, rye, barley, teff and buckwheat), pulses, all types of cabbage, cauliflower and broccoli, globe artichoke, Jerusalem artichoke, asparagus, celeriac, turnip, radish, salsify, dandelion greens, beetroot, onion, leek, garlic, plum, fig, date, apricot, apple, raw honey, molasses, linseed and psyllium husk.

Resistant starch: not all starch is created equal, some is easily digested and converted into glucose to fuel our body, and some (resistant starch) cannot be converted to glucose, but travels through the digestive system to feed the microbes in the large intestine. Resistant starch does not raise blood sugar and feeds the good microbes, so it is highly beneficial. The starch in rice, potatoes and wheat becomes fully digestible when freshly cooked, but if the cooked food is chilled, much of the starch becomes resistant again, even if heated briefly. To increase your starch intake, you just need to change the way that you prepare potatoes, pasta and rice to maximise the resistant starch they contain.

- **Rice:** cook rice in your usual way. Spread out on a tray to cool quickly and then transfer to the fridge for at least 3 hours. Eat within 36 hours either cold, as fried rice, or briefly reheat in a covered pan with a couple of tablespoons of water, allowing it to steam through. Alternatively, put into freezer bags, smooth flat and stack up in the freezer, so that you can have retrograded rice whenever you need it. Tap the bag with a rolling pin to loosen the grains if using straight from frozen and reheat as above, or put straight into a salad and allow to defrost completely.
- **Potatoes and pasta:** cook however you like and then chill for several hours or overnight. Eat cold as a salad, or reheat briefly.

Animal prebiotics: connective tissues (tendons, cartilage and skin) all contain fibre that may be almost as effective as soluble plant fibre at feeding the friendly microbes in your gut. While slow-cooked meat contains lots of gut-soothing collagen, you will get your animal fibre by gnawing on the soft ends of slow-cooked bones, eating the cartilaginous bits on the end of chicken wings and thighs, or eating tinned fish with bones. There may also be a small amount of prebiotic fibre in dry cured meats, such as prosciutto and salami, in addition to the probiotic qualities of cured meat.

Raw honey: raw honey is a source of prebiotic oligosaccharides and also contains beneficial enzymes that are mostly destroyed by heating, so look for raw or cold filtered honey and try to get something local.

NOURISHING FATS

Are some fats good and some fats bad? Yes, but probably not in the way you have been encouraged to think. Beneficial fats occur naturally in the food we eat, yet if they are processed in a way that damages them they become inflammatory because the chemical structure has been denatured. A good example of this would be a clear, flavourless vegetable oil, such as sunflower oil, which is processed using solvents and heat to extract the maximum amount of fat and ensure a long shelf life. The process works well for the manufacturer, but unfortunately damages the delicate polyunsaturated fats in the oil. Because the oil is also neutralised, bleached and deodorised during processing, you are unaware that anything is amiss. Anything made with this fat, such as margarine, mayonnaise, biscuits, salad dressings and ready meals, will contribute to inflammation in your cells and require you to consume more anti-inflammatory fat.

Polyunsaturated fats are most stable in the foods they naturally occur in; they soothe our immune system, nerves and skin, and we should aim to eat them every day in dark leafy greens, seeds, nuts, oily fish, seafood and wild meat. The essential fatty acid, omega-3, is particularly soothing and found in all the foods just mentioned.

Monounsaturated fats found in olive oil, avocado, nuts, grass-fed meat and game also have a soothing effect on gut mucosa, help to counter harmful bacteria, provide food for beneficial bacteria, and improve the ratio of good to bad cholesterol in your blood. Because monounsaturated oils, such as olive, rapeseed and avocado, are only moderately stable, it is ideal to eat them uncooked or only gently heated, so that they do not start to break down chemically. When fats are contained in a food, such as in meat or in a seed, they are partially protected from damage, so don't worry about roasting meat or toasting your seeds, just don't stir-fry in olive oil.

Saturated fats often get a bad press, but our bodies expect to find them in food and get disappointed if they are not there. We repair our cells with saturated fats and make vitamin D with it, so not having enough can be as bad as having too much. Despite what you might think, cholesterol in egg yolks, seafood, dairy products and meat can be beneficial in moderate amounts, helping to form the myelin sheath that surrounds every nerve in your body and supporting cell repair.

Duck fat, goose fat, chicken fat, lard and dripping all contain palmitoleic acid which helps reduce numbers of harmful bacteria in the gut, supporting immune function. Even butter can be a hero fat and not just because it makes crumpets taste so darned good! Butter contains butyric acid that can help restore the integrity of the gut mucosa, reduce inflammation and normalise cell function.

Make sure that you include fat in your diet because it will satisfy you, soothe you and help you thrive. To help you eat your fat in its most stable state, I have included a table of what to cook with below.

COOKING METHOD	TYPE OF FAT	THINGS TO AVOID
Deep-frying	Dripping, lard, coconut oil	Vegetable oils, vegetable shortening
Stir-frying, roasting meat, fish, potatoes or vegetables (over 140°C), searing meat, cooking steak or chops, sautéing over a higher heat, frying eggs	Beef dripping, lamb fat, coconut oil, lard, goose fat, duck fat, chicken fat, bacon fat. In moderation: cold-pressed sesame oil, peanut oil (groundnut oil)	Cooking sprays, vegetable shortening, vegetable oils
Slow-roasting vegetables, meat or fish (up to 140°C), softening onions or soffrito without colour, cooking pancakes or blinis, omelettes and scrambled eggs	Virgin olive oil, ghee, clarified butter, unsalted butter	Cooking sprays, clear vegetable oils, virgin rapeseed oil, margarine, spreadable butter
Avoid cooking. Good for dressing salads and vegetables, aïoli, dipping bread or drizzling over toast	The following cold-pressed (virgin) oils: almond, hazelnut, avocado, rapeseed, sunflower, macadamia, argan, hemp, borage, walnut	Margarine, shop-bought mayonnaise and salad dressings, unrefrigerated cold-pressed oils, refined vegetable oils

ANTI-INFLAMMATORY FOODS

There are two types of inflammation. General inflammation is what happens when you sprain your ankle or get stung by a wasp, and is characterised by local swelling, heat and redness. The cure is rest and ice and it is short lived and self-limiting. Systemic inflammation is what happens within the cells of our body when the most primitive part of our immune system (the innate immune system) releases pro-inflammatory cytokines (hormone-like substances) that ramp up the inflammatory activity of immune cells, and can result in cells not functioning as they should, or even in cell death, tissue damage or tumour formation. Many of the chronic diseases of modern life can be attributed to this.

Although some genetic conditions can influence your body's susceptibility for systemic inflammation, the best solution is to live and eat well. Certain things are known to increase inflammation, such as lack of sleep, shift working, lack of exercise, lack of sunlight, stress, dysbiosis (unbalanced gut microbiome), excessive intake of omega-6 polyunsaturated fats, damaged fats, alcohol or sugar.

In addition to eating a diverse range of the anti-inflammatory foods listed below, try to get out more, walk more, sing more and find ways to get the sun on your skin and a skip in your step. The blue light from electronic devices can mess with the natural rhythm of cortisol and melatonin production, so go to bed early and turn your phone off well before you hit the hay.

Fats: relying on foods that are high in omega-6, such as sunflower oil, corn oil, soya oil, poultry and grains, can cause inflammation because the ideal ratio of omega-3 to omega-6 (1:3) is skewed towards omega-6. Increase your omega-3 intake by eating the following foods and see Nourishing Fats (see page 17).

Herbs and spices: herbs pack the best nutritional punch of any plant food. I don't like to single any out too much, because the chances are if it tastes fragrant it will have an anti-inflammatory effect. The same goes for spices; chilli, cinnamon, cloves, cardamom, cumin, nigella and mustard are just a few with a great track record. Scatter Dukkah (see page 218), Gomasio (see page 214) and Shichimi Togarashi (see page 216) on your meals, and get creative with curries, chillies and laksas. Avoid using out-of-date herbs and spices as these can harbour mould.

Fruit: all fruit is fairly high in antioxidants, which encourage cell renewal and limit the damage caused by free radicals. The insoluble fibre in fruit helps the body to get rid of toxins created during cell metabolism, and the soluble fibre improves the microbiome, which regulates the immune response. As a rule, the brighter or darker the fruit, the more antioxidants it contains, but apples and pears are also great sources of soluble fibre. Fructose can be inflammatory in excess, such as in fruit juice or agave syrup, but whole fruit contains enough fibre to offset the fructose.

Fruit skins are particularly high in nutrients and citrus rind especially so. Adding Preserved Lemons (see page 203) and some citrus zest to meals not only powers up the flavour but will do you a power of good. Sea buckthorn is a native berry that grows wild in coastal areas and contains both high concentrations of soothing omega-9 (great for dry eyes and menopausal symptoms) and antioxidants. You can buy dried sea buckthorn to sprinkle over food, or gather it yourself if you are feeling intrepid.

Vegetables: if you want to calm your immune system, add more plants to your diet, especially vegetables. As with fruit, the brightly, deeply, dark-coloured vegetables contain the most antioxidants, but you should also be interested in the fibre content, as this will help you to excrete waste products and feed your microbiome, so celery, mushrooms and cauliflower rate highly, too.

Dark green leaves and avocados contain soothing

fats, while beets are rich with minerals that support cell function. The cabbage and onion families contain a good amount of sulphur, which helps cells to excrete the toxic by-products of metabolism. Tomatoes are rich in lycopene, which you can absorb better when they are cooked or fermented. I could find something good to say about most vegetables, so eat all of them, because they will keep you strong, healthy and vibrant.

Grains: grains are a mixed bag, health-wise. Refined grains, such as white rice and white flour, contain mostly starch and few nutrients. Whole grains are rich in nutrients that contribute to our wellbeing, but they also contain anti-nutrients that can interfere with digestion and absorption if eaten in large amounts. Fermenting transforms anti-nutrients, increasing the bioavailability of the good stuff contained in the germ of the grain, so eat sourdough bread, fermented porridges and pancakes and use sprouted flours where possible.

There are a couple of hero grains in terms of antioxidants; black rice is rich in anthocyanins, and buckwheat contains rutin, which is useful for vascular strength and repair.

Pulses (dried beans, peas and lentils): a fantastic source of fibre in our diets, pulses help to reduce our consumption of meat, too much of which can be inflammatory. However, they do contain high concentrations of substances called lectins (found in all plant foods), which can irritate the immune system and cause it to turn on itself. In order to minimise the lectin content of pulses, ideally cook them yourself: soak them in cold water overnight, boil rapidly for about 15 minutes in fresh water, drain and cook again in fresh water until tender. Pulses cooked this way can be frozen. Another method is to ferment your beans in some way (for example, Farinata, see page 117), or to eat them already fermented as tempeh or miso.

Meat: although meat fat on the whole has been considered inflammatory, it is likely that overconsumption of meat and underconsumption of vegetables is to blame. Wild game and meat from animals that have lived a natural life, rootling about with the sun on their backs, contain much higher levels of anti-inflammatory omega-3 fats than their barn-raised counterparts. The leaf lard fat (soft fat surrounding the kidneys and loin of the pig), so prized by the Italians and Spanish for charcuterie, has anti-inflammatory properties. Dissolved connective tissues and absorbable minerals that are present in Bone Broth (see page 53) make it a top anti-inflammatory addition to your diet, while traditionally cured meat makes a good occasional treat.

Fish: oily fish are a great source of long chain omega-3 fats. Depending on where they are reared, farmed fish can be exposed to high levels of antibiotics that find their way into your gut, and large fish can accumulate higher levels of heavy metals in their flesh than smaller fish. Mackerel, sardines and herrings make great anti-inflammatory meals, and anchovies a salty, savoury addition to anything from bolognaise sauce to roast lamb shoulder and salsa verde.

Seaweed: in addition to a rich complement of nourishing minerals, seaweeds contain a compound called fucoidan that has been shown to help formation of connective tissues and collagen and to reduce production of inflammatory cytokines (cytokines are proteins that are involved in cell signalling, but inflammatory cytokines can cause the immune system to become overactive). Both effects are particularly good for healing joint inflammation and reducing the swelling associated with seasonal allergies.

Make sure you eat nuts and seeds that are not rancid (you can taste when they are not fresh) and grind your linseed in a seed-dedicated coffee grinder as it can oxidise if stored for long, once it is ground.

Chocolate, wine, tea and coffee: it is a beguiling idea that our favourite treats are secretly good for us and we can carry on just as we were, but there are benefits to these after-dinner favourites. Cocoa powder, coffee, wine and tea all contain high levels of sirtuins, compounds that have been shown to reduce cell aging, reduce inflammation and improve cell detoxification. However, they also contain alcohol (wine), caffeine (chocolate, tea and coffee), theobromine (chocolate) and sugar (chocolate), compromising their anti-inflammatory benefits somewhat.

Moderate wine and (real) coffee drinkers have been shown to have a more diverse microbiome, but that could be due to some other factor that wasn't measured in the study. My advice is to eat and drink these treats moderately and to be aware that caffeine, theobromine or alcohol might not suit you if you are stressed, highly strung or fatigued. The benefits of cacao are much reduced when it is roasted, so raw chocolate (without agave syrup) is more beneficial than roasted. If you're looking to milk chocolate for your fix, there is barely enough of the good stuff in there to make it beneficial at all, so go as dark as you dare.

KITCHEN NOTES

Butter

I generally use salted butter to cook with, except for frying, where I use unsalted butter for gentle frying, or ghee or clarified butter for a slightly higher heat. I love lactic butter, which is lightly fermented for an extra buttery flavour and is virtually lactose free.

Citrus fruit

I use unwaxed citrus in recipes that call for zest. If you are including citrus fruit in a ferment or in water kefir, it is important to choose organic fruit, as any chemicals present in the skin could interfere with the growth of beneficial bacteria.

Dairy-free ingredients

If you can tolerate it, there is absolutely nothing wrong with dairy milk and I recommend that you go for organic, if you can. However, if you are looking for dairy alternatives and do not have the time to make your own (see Almond Milk, page 237), there are many milks, yoghurts and ice creams made from nuts, seeds, coconut, rice or oats. Most of my recipes will work just fine with a straight swap from dairy to a non-dairy alternative, although you may need to adjust the quantity. When substituting coconut oil, olive oil or another pure fat for butter, use 20 per cent less.

Dairy alternatives that contain any of the following ingredients may have a negative impact on gut health, so try to avoid these completely: carrageenan, hydroxypropyl methylcellulose (HMC), mono- and diglycerides of fatty acids.

If you have sensitive digestion, limit consumption of the following: gellan gum, xanthan gum, guar gum and soya lecithin. It is also wise to avoid added fructose, agave syrup and fructose-glucose syrup, as these can be inflammatory. As with most things, it is the dose that matters, so don't worry if you only consume these products very occasionally.

Eggs

All the recipes in this book call for medium-sized organic eggs, unless large eggs are specified.

Fermenting

The lacto-fermented recipes in this book use salt to retard harmful bacteria and encourage the growth of lactic acid-forming bacteria. It is counterproductive to sterilise or sanitise anything involved in the process, whether it be hands, surfaces, jars, bottles or rubber seals. Just give everything a good wash with hot soapy water and rinse well, for your ferment to keep itself fresh and germ-free (as long as you give it the right conditions to thrive).

It is important to exclude as much air as possible from the surface of your ferment to minimise mould growth while it is maturing. I use a weight in the form of a ziplock freezer bag filled with either water, brine (10g/⅓oz of salt to 500ml/18fl oz of water), clean pebbles, clean coins or baking beans to weigh down the vegetables in the ferment and keep them under the brine. To do this, just press an open medium-sized ziplock freezer bag onto the top of the ferment and fill (as above) until you can see the brine from the ferment above the vegetables, then zip the bag, close the jar (without its rubber seal) and leave to ferment at room temperature (between 18–20°C is ideal) for the time given in the recipe. Because ferments produce gas while they mature, you may find that a little liquid comes up over the top of the jar while it ferments, so I put my jars on a plate or tray to catch anything that overflows.

Once the ferment is ready, transfer it to smaller storage jars (again, no need to sterilise), and if it is a kraut- or kimchi-style ferment, press the vegetables down firmly using clean fingers or the end of a rolling pin, so that the juices come to the top of the ferment. For a brine ferment, include a ziplock freezer bag weight (as above) to keep the vegetables under the brine if necessary, and refrigerate.

When ferments are stored this way, they will keep fresh for many months, whether the jar is opened or not (approximate storage times are given for each recipe). Use clean implements to get the ferment out of the jar and press or weight everything down again after you have finished using it.

A large jar and a ziplock freezer bag are the only essentials you need for fermenting, but you may like to buy extra kit if you enjoy preserving things in this way. Airlocks are available for preserving jars that prevent bugs getting in, but allow gas to escape, although I would still use a weight to keep everything under the brine. Stoppered glass bottles are ideal if you plan to make Water Kefir (see page 239), although screw-cap bottles work, too. See Useful Suppliers on page 248.

Fish

If you are unsure about which fish are sustainable where you live, look for an online list, such as the Marine Stewardship Council (www.msc.org), and choose fish that is sustainably caught or responsibly farmed.

Herbs

Herbs can be grown in pots on a windowsill or outside, or in a small patch of your garden, and they are packed with flavour and nutrients. All of the herbs in this book are fresh except bay leaves, which can be used fresh or dried.

Linseeds

Linseeds and flax are interchangeable names for the same thing. I buy golden linseeds and grind small

amounts in a coffee grinder that I don't use for anything strongly flavoured (like spices). It tastes better, costs less and can be ground more finely than purchased ground linseed. Ground linseed oxidises quickly, so keep any unused ground seeds in a closed jar in the fridge for up to a fortnight.

Meat and poultry

You are what you eat and therefore it matters where and how the meat you eat is reared. I choose to eat free-range (or wild) and preferably organically raised meat and poultry, because it tends to have a much healthier fat profile (not lower in fat, but with better ratios of good fat), more flavour and is less likely to be treated with antibiotics or hormones during its life. We all know that we should be eating less meat, so think about reducing your portion size and going for higher welfare when you do eat it.

Oils

The oils used in this book are always cold-pressed or virgin (the meaning is the same), so that they are eaten in the most stable state, with minimal industrial intervention. Use virgin olive oil for all the recipes in the book that call for olive oil and do not heat beyond the most gentle sauté. I also use cold-pressed sunflower oil and occasionally cold-pressed rapeseed oil for their softer, nutty flavours, but do not cook with these due to their higher polyunsaturated fat content, as this is damaged by heat.

Oven temperatures

When I am baking cakes or pastry, I tend to use a fan-assisted oven, but for most other recipes I use a conventional non-fan oven because I find that this gives crisper skin on meat and fish, and better roast spuds and root veg. As ovens vary so much, I use an inexpensive oven thermometer to ensure the temperature is right.

Seaweed

Seaweeds are incredibly rich in minerals and can be foraged or bought dried in the shops. Arame and wakame are good introductions to the world of seaweed as they are delicately flavoured, and kombu (kelp) is brilliant for adding gut-friendly glutamine to vegetable stock. If you love the flavour of seaweed, then add small amounts to your meals as often as you like. See Useful Suppliers (page 248) for suppliers of seaweed.

Vegetable and fruit preparation

Because peels tend to be incredibly nutritious, I would encourage you to leave the skin on as many vegetables and fruit as you can and simply wash off any visible soil using cold water and a vegetable brush. The only real exceptions to this rule are: onions and garlic, vegetables and fruit with coarse skin, such as pineapple, celeriac, salsify and some types of squash, or vegetables that you are using to make a fine-textured mash or purée. I also tend to peel older carrots if I am fermenting them as the skin can darken or turn bitter – young carrots are fine with their peel. Fresh berries, such as strawberries and raspberries, are best washed only briefly just before you eat them, and mushrooms become soggy if washed (just remove any loose dirt with a soft brush).

Yoghurt, crème fraîche and milk kefir

Many recipes in the book use live yoghurt, crème fraîche or milk kefir as probiotic additions to a meal, or to take advantage of the beneficial bacteria they contain to ferment porridges and batters and make them more digestible. I generally use a live, creamy Greek-style yoghurt, live full-fat crème fraîche or whole milk kefir, so if you choose low-fat varieties, the recipe may turn out slightly different in some cases. To find live dairy products, look for one of these words on the packet: bio, live, lactic cultures, Lactobacillus, streptococcus, bifidus.

CALM

BREAKFASTS

OATMEAL HOTCAKES WITH BLUEBERRIES AND CRÈME FRAÎCHE

GENTLE VEGETABLE HASH

SOOTHING PORRIDGE

BLACK RICE PORRIDGE WITH CASHEW CREAM

SOURDOUGH CRUMPETS

GLUTEN-FREE OR RYE SOURDOUGH STARTER

BIRCHER MUESLI

MILLET PORRIDGE WITH PEACH AND BLACKBERRIES

AUBERGINE CAVIAR WITH PERFECT POACHED EGGS AND SMOKY BUTTER

COURGETTE CAVIAR WITH SOURDOUGH TOAST AND A FRIED EGG

HAPPY TUMMY GRANOLA

Start the day with a soothing breakfast and the chances are that your belly will behave better for the rest of the day. Because our feelings influence our guts so profoundly, your routine could also focus on calming the anxiety that many people feel when faced with a busy day of work.

It helps to think about breakfast well in advance and most of the recipes in this chapter can be made the day before, so that all you need to do is heat up a bowl of creamy porridge or poach an egg before you sit down to a proper breakfast in the morning.

OATMEAL HOTCAKES WITH BLUEBERRIES AND CRÈME FRAÎCHE

Serves 4

These soothingly buttery hotcakes are wholesome without being heavy, due to whisked egg whites and a light touch with the folding. Cook them slowly to avoid burning the butter and then pile them up on a pretty plate and allow everyone to help themselves to crème fraîche, fruit or maybe a drizzle of local raw honey. Leftover hotcakes freeze really well and just need a little warming through under the grill.

50g (2oz) unsalted butter, plus extra for frying

4 organic eggs, separated

100g (4oz) buckwheat flour

50g (2oz) fine oatmeal or porridge oats

100g (4oz) live Greek-style yoghurt

2 teaspoons baking powder

Pinch of sea salt

TO SERVE

350g (12oz) blueberries

200g (7oz) crème fraîche (or 300g/11oz live Greek-style yoghurt)

Raw honey or maple syrup

Melt the butter, then leave it to cool for a few minutes while you weigh out your other ingredients. Whisk the egg whites until stiff and set aside briefly while you beat everything else together in a separate bowl using the same whisk. Fold the egg whites gently into the batter, until no lumps of egg white are showing but the mixture is still light and airy.

Set a heavy-based frying pan over a low heat to warm through for a few minutes, then grease with butter using a heatproof brush or some kitchen paper folded tightly and secured with a clothes peg.

Place dessertspoonfuls of batter evenly in the pan, leaving room to get a palette knife in to turn them. Cook for a few minutes, watching the bubbles form on the surface. If you like, you can scatter some of the blueberries into each hotcake while the batter is still soft, to make blueberry hotcakes.

When the underneath is deep golden and the edges just firm to the touch, carefully flip the hotcakes over using a palette knife and your fingers. Cook on the other side for 30 seconds, just until set underneath. Check to see if they are done by tapping with your fingertips – there should be no squidge, but if they feel completely solid, they might be a bit overdone. Keep your hotcakes warm while you repeat with the remaining batter, until it is all used up.

Pile the hotcakes onto a pretty plate, bring the blueberries, crème fraîche and honey or syrup to the table and then tuck in.

GENTLE VEGETABLE HASH

Serves 2

Vegetables make a great choice for breakfast, bringing you closer to that 8-portion a day goal with ease. If you need some protein with your veg, add an egg, some cured fish like gravadlax or a little good-quality salami. As your gut improves, think about slowly adding more challenging vegetables to this mix, like onions, garlic, broccoli, cabbage, globe artichoke hearts, dandelion leaves or even a handful of cooked beans or chickpeas. I like to stir a large spoonful of hummus through mine for extra prebiotic creaminess.

2 courgettes

250g (9oz) sweet potato or squash

2 teaspoons duck fat, salted butter or other heat-stable fat

1 garlic clove, squashed but left intact (or finely chop, if you plan to eat it)

2 handfuls of fresh or frozen peas (or fresh or frozen broad beans)

2 handfuls of soft salad leaves, rinsed and patted dry

2 tablespoons tahini or Sunflower Seed Butter (see page 124)

Juice of ½ lemon

Sea salt

Scrub the courgettes and sweet potato or squash, peel if you struggle to digest the fibrous peels (always peel squash unless it is a very thin-skinned variety) and cut into 1–2cm (½–¾in) dice.

Melt the fat in a large frying pan or saucepan over a low heat, then add the diced vegetables and garlic and sauté gently for about 10–15 minutes, until they are soft and just starting to catch some colour. Add the peas (or broad beans) to the pan and sauté until they are cooked through but still bright green, stirring frequently.

Divide the salad leaves between two large dining bowls. Remove the garlic clove and discard (if left whole), stir the tahini or sunflower seed butter into the hot vegetables, then season well with salt and a good squeeze of lemon juice. Stir so that everything is coated, pile on top of the leaves and tuck in.

SOOTHING PORRIDGE

Per person quantities

Setting a moment aside in the evening to soak your oats gives porridge a creamier texture, rounder flavour and makes for an almost instant breakfast the next day. If you can find jumbo oats or even pinhead oatmeal, these give more texture to your porridge. Soaking with live yoghurt reduces anti-nutrients that interfere with digestion, raw milk contains beneficial enzymes, and collagen powder helps to soothe the lining of the small intestine. Quantities for additions are given as a guide only, so simply adjust to suit your taste.

80g (3oz) oats

2 tablespoons ground almonds or sunflower or pumpkin seeds

1 heaped teaspoon live natural yoghurt

275ml (9½fl oz) tepid water

Pinch of sea salt (optional)

Raw milk or home-made Nut Milk (see page 237) (optional)

2 tablespoons collagen powder (optional)

TO SERVE

2–3 tablespoons live natural yoghurt or coconut yoghurt

Large handful of fresh fruit

Small handful of flaked almonds or chopped nuts

2–3 teaspoons ground linseed

Ground cinnamon, to taste

1 teaspoon raw honey, Manuka honey or date or maple syrup (optional)

Put the oats and ground almonds or ground seeds into a jar or bowl and stir in the yoghurt and tepid water. Cover and leave at room temperature for 12–24 hours.

In the morning, transfer the porridge to a small pan, add the salt (if using) and cook gently until the oats are soft, stirring often to prevent sticking. You may need to add more liquid (raw or nut milk or water, depending on taste) as it is absorbed by the oats – add enough to get the right consistency for you and cook until the oats are very soft, about 3–4 minutes. Take off the heat and stir in the collagen powder (if using).

Serve topped with the yoghurt (or a dash of milk), fresh fruit, flaked almonds or chopped nuts, ground linseed and a good sprinkle of cinnamon. Add the honey or syrup if the porridge tastes too sour.

With all the additions (to serve), the porridge part of your bowl should be between ⅓–½ of a bowlful. If you find that the amount given here is too much for you, simply heat up the leftovers the next day, or adjust the quantities down to suit.

BLACK RICE PORRIDGE WITH CASHEW CREAM

Serves 4

Black rice (riso nerone) is an incredibly dark-coloured short grain variety from Italy, which contains high levels of antioxidant anthocyanins that give the grain its deep purplish-black colour. It has a sweet, nutty flavour and satisfying chewy texture that makes for a very sustaining breakfast. You can also try this with other varieties, such as red Camargue rice or short grain brown rice. Add some seasonal fruit, a creamy cashew nut swirl and you will fairly skip to work afterwards!

FOR THE RICE

2 teaspoons salted butter

400g (14oz) black rice (or red Camargue rice or short grain brown rice)

1.2 litres (2 pints) boiling water

Pinch of sea salt

50g (2oz) ground almonds

Seeds from 8 green cardamom pods

4 teaspoons raw honey

80g (3oz) shelled pistachio nuts (or hazelnuts for low FODMAP), chopped

4 ripe figs (or other seasonal fruit)

FOR THE CASHEW CREAM

4 tablespoons cashew butter

4 teaspoons raw honey

Pinch of sea salt

For the rice, melt the butter in a large pan over a low heat and when it starts to foam a little, add the rice and cook for 30 seconds, stirring constantly. Pour in the boiling water, add the salt and ground almonds and bring back to the boil. Cover and simmer gently, stirring occasionally, until the rice is juicily soft and the texture of a creamy porridge, about 30–40 minutes. You may need to add more water. Scrape out into a large bowl and spread up the sides so it will cool quickly, then chill in the fridge for at least 2 hours and up to 24 hours.

When you are ready to eat, grind the cardamom seeds to a fine powder, then stir this into the rice with the honey and three-quarters of the pistachios. Pile the rice into pretty bowls, slice the figs and arrange on top.

To make the cashew cream, simply stir together the cashew butter, honey and salt and then whisk in enough cold water, a tablespoon at a time, until the sauce is the texture of double cream. Drizzle the cashew cream over the rice and figs and scatter with the remaining pistachios. You can use tahini or a different nut butter as an alternative.

SOURDOUGH CRUMPETS

Makes 8–9

Whenever I bake sourdough bread, these crumpets are the inevitable chef's treat, as they use the discarded feed from my sourdough starter. Because the bacteria in the starter have been munching away on the anti-nutrients in the flour, these are nourishing and digestible as well as being delicious. Tender and deeply flavoursome, they are worth making a starter for even if you don't plan to bake bread. I mean, who needs bread when you have crumpets? Crumpet rings are essential.

About 2 tablespoons unsalted butter or duck or bacon fat

500g (1lb 2oz) active Sourdough Starter (see pages 35–37)

2 pinches of sea salt

1 teaspoon light or dark muscovado sugar (optional)

½ teaspoon bicarbonate of soda

8 crumpet rings

Heat a heavy-based, dry frying pan over a medium heat until moderately hot. Ideally use two pans, so you can cook all the mixture at once. Generously smear the insides of the crumpet rings with a little of the butter or fat and set aside for a moment.

Pour the sourdough starter into a jug and whisk in the salt and sugar (if using). Dissolve the bicarbonate of soda in 1½ teaspoons of cold water and then briefly whisk this into the starter for no more than 15 seconds.

Pop the crumpet rings into the hot pan(s) and put ½ teaspoon of butter or fat into each one. Let the fat melt (this will only take a couple of seconds or so), then pour the starter mixture into the rings, dividing it evenly, until each one is about three-quarters full. Turn the heat down to medium-low and let the crumpets cook, until most of the top is starting to set but is not quite cooked in the middle, about 4–5 minutes.

Carefully use tongs or some folded kitchen paper to pick up the hot rings and lift them off the crumpets in the pan. Use a palette knife to lift and gently turn the crumpets over without burning your fingers. Cook for 1–2 minutes on the other side and then remove to a wire rack to cool a little before serving.

Eat straight away, while still warm, or cool, then freeze for up to a month and toast from frozen, sprinkled with a little water first.

GLUTEN-FREE OR RYE SOURDOUGH STARTER

In addition to baking my own gluten-free sourdough bread, I use a sourdough starter to ferment pancakes, breakfast muffins, crumpets, pastry and farinata. You can make a gluten-free starter using any whole grain gluten-free flour, or use rye, spelt, emmer or einkorn flour if you can tolerate gluten. For more information on why sourdough is good for you, see page 20. For gluten-free sourdough bread recipes, see my book, *River Cottage Gluten Free*. Follow the method below to make your starter in five days and then you can use it and keep it dormant in the fridge between bakes for years. Read the notes on pages 36–37 before you get started.

DAY 1

120g (4½oz) brown rice flour or rye flour
180g (6oz) lukewarm filtered or mineral water
(use 240g/9oz for rye flour)
Small bunch of unwashed red or white grapes
(optional) or Pear Water (see page 36)

Mix the flour and water together in a bowl, nestle the grapes in (if using), then cover with a clean cloth and leave in a warm place. Your starter likes it a bit warmer than you do, so between 24–28°C is ideal (such as an airing cupboard or quite near a radiator). If your house is colder than this, you may find that you struggle to get your starter going and end up with a very sour, but not bubbly mixture. This is because yeasts like warmth, whereas the lactic bacteria thrive at slightly lower temperatures. See also the 'Too warm?' notes on page 37.

DAY 2

120g (4½oz) brown rice flour or rye flour
180g (6oz) lukewarm filtered or mineral water
(use 240g/9oz for rye flour)

Lift out the grapes, then add the flour and water 'feed', whisk vigorously to mix, replace the grapes, cover and return to a warm place.

DAY 3

240g (9oz) brown rice flour or rye flour
320g (11½oz) lukewarm filtered or mineral water
(use 480g/1lb 1oz for rye flour)

Lift out the grapes, then add the flour and water 'feed', whisk vigorously to mix, replace the grapes, cover and return to a warm place.

DAY 4 MORNING

300g (11oz) brown rice flour or rye flour
400g (14oz) cold filtered or mineral water (use 600g/1lb 5oz for rye flour)

By now the sourdough starter should have started to bubble and smell a little yeasty. Take out the grapes, squeeze them a little to release a small amount of juice and then discard the grapes. Whisk the starter vigorously, then weigh out 700g (1lb 9oz) of the starter (900g/2lb for rye). (Discard the remainder or make pancakes or crumpets with it.) Whisk the flour and water 'feed' into the starter, cover again and return to a warm place.

DAY 4 EVENING

Before bed, whisk the starter vigorously and weigh out 700g (1lb 9oz) again (900g/2lb for rye) (discard the remainder) and feed it as for Day 4 morning (using the same fresh quantities of flour and water 'feed'). Cover again and return to a warm place.

DAY 5 MORNING

Whisk the starter vigorously and weigh out 700g (1lb 9oz) of the starter again (900g/2lb for rye) and discard the remainder as before, then feed it as for Day 4 morning (using the same fresh quantities of flour and water 'feed'). Cover again and leave in a warm place to bubble up for 2–3 hours (4–5 hours for rye).

It should now be ready to bake with and this is referred to as an 'active' starter. If it doesn't seem powerful enough, whisk and weigh out 700g (1lb 9oz) of the starter again (900g/2lb for rye) and discard the remainder as before, then feed it again (with the same quantities of flour and water given for Day 4 morning) every 6–8 hours.

Each time you feed it, you must weigh out 700g (1lb 9oz) of the starter again (900g/2lb for rye) and discard the rest, otherwise your kitchen will overflow with starter. If you plan to bake large batches of bread, increase your reserve accordingly.

WHICH FLOUR TO USE?

Rice flour works well for a gluten-free sourdough starter because it has a mild flavour and is cheap to maintain. You need to use brown rice flour, or at the very least a rice flour with some brown rice in it. This is because the yeasts and bacteria that will come to life and flourish when you give them heat and water, live on the brown part (germ) of the grain. Teff, sorghum, millet, buckwheat and quinoa flour can be great to give a starter a kick-start, too – all are yeasty and more sour than rice flour. If you like the flavour, you could switch to a mixture of rice and another flour for all feeds. For a gluten starter, rye makes a great start and then you can change the flavour once it is established by adding other ancient grain flours such as spelt, einkorn or emmer.

WATER

Always use filtered or mineral water for starting and maintaining your starter, because chlorine is the enemy of yeast and bacteria. If you don't have access to either, leave some tap water out for 24 hours, uncovered, to allow the chlorine to evaporate and then use this to feed your starter.

HOW MUCH TO FEED MY STARTER?

The ratio for a gluten-free sourdough starter is three parts flour to four parts water. For a rye starter, the ratio is one part flour to two parts water. The consistency of the starter, if fed like this, should look like lightly whipped double cream. You need to double the starter each time you feed it. I keep a reservoir of 700g (1lb 9oz) of gluten-free starter in my fridge at home, and each time I feed it I give it 300g (11oz) of flour and 400g (14oz) of water (keep 900g/2lb for a rye starter and feed it 300g/11oz of flour and 600g/1lb 5oz of water). When I am finished baking, I pour off 700g (1lb 9oz) of starter and keep this in the fridge until the next time – anything left over (called 'discard') can be used to make pancakes and crumpets, or to give the compost a kick-start.

PEAR WATER

If you make your starter in the winter, a pear might be more appropriate than grapes. Grate a whole pear (peel, core and all), then put it into a soup bowl and pour over just enough filtered or mineral (chlorine-free) water to cover. Cover the bowl and leave at room temperature for 12–24 hours. Strain and use the water for days 1 and 2 of making your starter, or to boost a less than bubbly starter.

WATER KEFIR

When my starter has been resting in the fridge, I sometimes use Water Kefir (see page 239) as the liquid part of the feed, and find that this gives it a real lift and makes it very vigorous and yeasty. This will not work with milk kefir, so make sure you buy the correct grains and use the liquid kefir that you brew from them to feed your starter, not the grains themselves.

TOO WARM?

The back of the Aga or on a radiator is too warm for a starter. If your starter bubbles up nicely on days 1 and 2, but seems lifeless on day 3 or 4, the chances are it burnt itself out because it was warm but didn't have enough food to keep chomping. If this is the case, feed your starter twice daily from day 3 until it is well established on day 5 or 6. Each time you feed it, for gluten free, weigh out 700g (1lb 9oz) of the starter mixture and feed this with 300g (11oz) of flour and 400g (14oz) of water, discarding the extra starter, or using it to make pancakes or crumpets. (For rye starter, weigh out 900g/2lb and feed it with 300g/11oz of flour and 600g/1lb 5oz of water.)

HOW DO YOU KNOW WHEN IT'S READY?

Your starter is ready when it starts to bubble up within a couple of hours of feeding (4–6 hours for a rye starter); this may take a little longer if it has been dormant in the fridge. It should rise up in the bowl, take on a bubbly mousse-like texture and even bubble and pop as though it is alive! You may find that your new starter is not as vigorous as a well established one and in this case, to avoid disappointment, you can add a little fresh or fast-action dried yeast to your loaf to give it a bit of extra lift. Between 6–9g (⅛–¼oz) of fresh yeast or 2–3g (¹⁄₁₆oz) of fast-action dried yeast will give you a lift, without taking over. Then you can add some of the kick-starters listed above to try and strengthen the yeast population in your starter.

CAN I USE IT STRAIGHT AWAY ON DAY 5?

Yes! After you have fed it and it has risen up and looks bubbly and alive, you can go straight on to bake your first loaf or make a batch of crumpets, but bear in mind it may still be a little weak. If you don't want to bake with it that day, put it into a clean, lidded plastic container and keep it in the fridge. If you want to use a Kilner jar, take the rubber seal out first, so any gas can escape.

AFTER IT HAS BEEN IN THE FRIDGE?

Remember to warm up your starter after it has been in the fridge. Feed the starter, whisk well, put the bowl into lukewarm water and cover with a clean cloth for 2–3 hours (4–5 hours for rye); it should then be bubbly and 'active'. If your starter isn't coming to life, you may need to give it up to 24 hours to wake up. Feed it again in 8–12 hours, and then again another 8–12 hours later before using.

BIRCHER MUESLI

Per person quantities

Swiss doctor, Maximilian Bircher-Benner created his eponymous muesli in the 19th century when people were more likely to start the day with half a ham hock and a pint of small beer than some oats. Oats contain anti-nutrients that can be reduced by soaking with live yoghurt and they are also easier to digest once hydrated. Although delicious and very traditional when made with grated raw apple, use any seasonal fruit that you can happily tolerate. Almonds and hazelnuts are easy to digest, but as you start to challenge your gut and introduce new foods, think about including sunflower seeds, pumpkin seeds and pistachios for their additional fibre content. Dried berry powders are available online and in some supermarkets and provide a brilliant hit of vitamin C and other antioxidants.

35g (1¼oz) jumbo oats

15g (½oz) almonds or hazelnuts, chopped

1 heaped tablespoon live natural yoghurt, coconut yoghurt or milk kefir, plus extra to serve

25g (1oz) flaked almonds

75g (3oz) fresh raspberries (or a grated apple or other fresh berries)

1 tablespoon ground linseed

Dried sea buckthorn or other berry powder, to taste (optional)

Ground cinnamon, milk and raw honey, to serve

Put the oats, chopped nuts and yoghurt or milk kefir in a bowl, pour in enough cold water just to cover and stir well. Cover with a plate and leave overnight at room temperature.

Toast the flaked almonds in a dry frying pan over a medium heat for a few minutes, moving constantly until they are pale gold, and then tip into a bowl to cool until the morning. You can do enough for a week in one go if you might eat this every day (just store in an airtight container).

In the morning, add 50g (2oz) of the raspberries (or a grated apple for a higher FODMAP breakfast) and a couple of dessertspoons of yoghurt or milk kefir and stir to incorporate. Sprinkle with the ground linseed, toasted flaked almonds, dried berry powder (if using) and cinnamon. Pour a little milk around the edge, top with the remaining raspberries and drizzle no more than a teaspoon of honey on top, then serve.

MILLET PORRIDGE WITH PEACH AND BLACKBERRIES

Per person quantities

As autumn draws closer and the mornings have a little sharpness to them, I start to think about having porridge again. Soaked millet makes a satisfyingly creamy porridge, with a lovely nubbly texture and a high phosphorus and glutamic acid content that makes it an excellent choice to repair the gut lining. A little extra gut healing comes from some collagen powder – an excellent addition if your gut needs soothing. Peaches are at the height of their loveliness in September, but later in the year choose apples and pears. If you are sensitive to fructose, try rhubarb, raspberries, bananas, blueberries, strawberries or papaya, depending on the time of year.

80g (3oz) millet grain

1 teaspoon live natural yoghurt

200ml (7fl oz) tepid water

Small pinch of sea salt

15g (½oz) unsalted butter

125–150ml (4–5fl oz) milk (or milk alternative)

2 tablespoons collagen powder (optional)

TO SERVE

1 ripe peach

2–3 tablespoons live natural yoghurt or coconut yoghurt

Large handful of fresh blackberries

Raw honey, to drizzle

Put the millet into a jar or bowl and stir in the yoghurt and water. Cover and leave at room temperature for around 24 hours.

In the morning, transfer the porridge to a small pan, add the salt and cook gently, stirring often, for about 10–15 minutes, until the millet grains are tender and most of the liquid is absorbed. You may need to add more liquid if the millet grains are not quite tender. Add the butter and milk and cook gently, stirring constantly, until the porridge is a creamy consistency – don't let it boil if you are using dairy milk, as this will taint the flavour. Take off the heat and stir in the collagen powder (if using).

If your peach is a little firm, try slicing it and griddling the pieces to give them a caramel flavour and those lovely charred lines. Serve the porridge topped with live yoghurt, peach slices, a scatter of blackberries and a drizzle of honey.

AUBERGINE CAVIAR WITH PERFECT POACHED EGGS AND SMOKY BUTTER

Serves 4

Make aubergine caviar on a lazy Sunday, so that you can have this for breakfast during the week. The caviar is also great as part of a mezze meal, or for dipping crunchy carrots into. My method for cooking poached eggs takes all the anxiety out of getting it right, allowing you to cradle a mug of tea and gently ease into the day.

3 aubergines, cut into small dice

75ml (3fl oz) Garlic Oil (see page 225)

3 pinches of sea salt

Juice of 1 lemon, or to taste

TO SERVE

8 rashers streaky bacon

4 organic eggs, at room temperature

4 Teff and Sesame Pancakes (see page 122), warmed

Live natural yoghurt or Tahini Sauce (see page 224) (optional)

Handful of flat-leaf parsley, chopped

Smoky Butter (see page 227), warmed (optional)

Put the aubergines into a pan with the garlic oil and salt. Cook gently for about 45 minutes, stirring occasionally, until the aubergines break down completely and start to catch a little on the bottom of the pan. Leave to cool completely, then add enough lemon juice so it tastes lemony but is not mouth-puckering. Scrape into a jar, cover and keep in the fridge until you need it.

When you are ready to serve, cook the streaky bacon in a dry frying pan until it is golden brown on both sides, then drain on kitchen paper.

Meanwhile, bring a large pan of water to the boil. Crack an egg into a cup and then tip into a fine mesh sieve over a bowl to allow any loose egg white to drain away. Turn the pan of water down as low as it can go so the water doesn't even tremble, lower the egg into it and roll it out of the sieve. Repeat with the other three eggs, then move them around by stirring the water gently as they cook for about 4 minutes, until the white is set but the yolk is still runny. Remove with a slotted spoon and rest briefly on kitchen paper.

Spread the warm pancakes with a generous helping of aubergine caviar, add a dollop of yoghurt or tahini sauce (for a dairy-free option), if you like, and sprinkle with parsley, then loosely fold into quarters. Top each one with a poached egg and a couple of bacon rashers, then drizzle the warm smoky butter (or more tahini sauce, if using) over everything, Jackson Pollock-style.

COURGETTE CAVIAR WITH SOURDOUGH TOAST AND A FRIED EGG

Serves 4

I have a huge patch of courgettes growing in my garden and they are prolific during the summer, so we end up eating them most days. If you cook courgettes long and slow in olive oil, they take on a creamy baba ganoush quality that makes a quick and delicious breakfast piled on toast and topped with an egg. The secret is to make a big batch of courgette caviar in advance and just warm it through in the morning. If you don't have lemon balm or fennel, try dill, tarragon, oregano or basil leaves instead. As your digestion improves, think about adding a finely chopped garlic clove to the caviar, then increase the amount as you tolerate it better.

100ml (3½fl oz) Garlic Oil (see page 225)

2kg (4½lb) courgettes, chopped into small dice

1 garlic clove, finely chopped (optional)

Finely grated zest of 2 lemons, plus juice of ½–1 lemon

3–4 pinches of sea salt

2–3 heads of herb fennel flowers or handful of herb fennel fronds

Small handful of lemon balm leaves, chopped (optional)

Large handful of mint leaves, chopped

4 large organic eggs, fried in lard or poached

4 large or 8 small slices of sourdough bread

Pour the garlic oil into a large lidded pan and set over a low heat. Add the courgettes, garlic (if using) and lemon zest, sprinkle in the salt, then put the lid on and cook slowly for at least an hour, stirring occasionally, until the courgettes have almost dissolved into each other and the bottom is catching a little. Give it more time rather than turn up the heat if the courgettes are stubbornly firm. The final result should be creamy and jammy, with a subtle sweetness from the slow cooking.

Pull the fennel flowers from the heads or chop the fronds. When the courgettes are completely soft, take off the heat and stir in all the herbs, then add lemon juice according to taste. Check if the mixture needs a little more salt, then set aside while you fry or poach the eggs to your liking (see Aubergine Caviar recipe opposite for how to poach eggs) and toast the bread.

Pile some courgette caviar on the toast and top each with a cooked egg. I like to scatter mine with some Fennel Dukkah (see page 218) and finish with a drizzle of Tahini Sauce (see page 224).

Any extra courgette caviar will keep for at least a week packed into a clean jar with olive oil poured on top to exclude the air. Keep it in the fridge and reheat gently before serving.

HAPPY TUMMY GRANOLA

*Makes about 1.3kg (3lb) — servings depend on how much you eat and how you use it
(i.e. as a complete breakfast or as a sprinkle)*

Soaking prebiotic porridge oats with a little live natural yoghurt helps to reduce the anti-nutrients that can interfere with digestion. Once baked, the oats develop a deeply toasty flavour that is very moreish. Cinnamon, vanilla, a little syrup and a handful of raisins sweeten things up without upsetting your blood sugar. Leave out the raisins, increase the syrup a little and eat with fresh fruit if you struggle to digest dried fruit.

100g (4oz) coconut oil, or 50g (2oz) lard or duck fat, or 100g (4oz) unsalted butter

800g (1¾lb) porridge oats – jumbo oats work best

150ml (¼ pint) olive oil

4 tablespoons live natural yoghurt

4 teaspoons vanilla extract

50g (2oz) date or maple syrup or carob molasses

4 teaspoons ground cinnamon

150g (5oz) sunflower or pumpkin seeds

100g (4oz) flaked almonds or chopped hazelnuts

150g (5oz) raisins or chopped un-sulphured dried fruit

The day before you bake the granola, melt the hard fat and let it cool until just warm, then put the porridge oats into a large mixing bowl with the olive oil, yoghurt, vanilla extract, syrup or molasses and 400ml (14fl oz) water and mix with a wooden spoon. Pour the cooled melted fat onto the oat mixture and mix until all the oats are sticky. Cover and leave at room temperature for 12–24 hours.

Preheat the oven to 160°C/140°C fan/gas 3. Tip the oat mixture onto 2 baking trays and break it up into smaller lumps that roughly cover each tray. Bake for 30 minutes and then turn the oaty clumps using a fork. Bake for a further 1½–2 hours this way, turning the granola over every 30 minutes. The granola should be almost completely dry when it is ready, but not too golden.

Sprinkle 2 teaspoons of the cinnamon over each tray of granola and mix it in. Add the seeds and nuts now if you like them toasted (just divide them evenly between each tray and mix in). Turn the oven up to 180°C/160°C fan/gas 4 and bake the granola for another 15 minutes, until completely crisp and toasty with a deep golden tinge.

Leave to cool completely on the trays, then tip into a mixing bowl and add the dried fruit (and seeds and nuts, if not added earlier), mixing well to distribute. Store in an airtight container for up to a month.

SOUPS

MINTY PEA AND WATERCRESS SOUP WITH MILK KEFIR

ROAST TOMATO SOUP WITH CRÈME FRAÎCHE AND BEET KVASS

NANA'S CHICKEN SOUP

BONE BROTH

MISO SOUP WITH RIBBON PICKLE

Soup is the ideal thing to heal and restore a troubled gut, as the long, slow simmering makes nutrients more available and breaks down elements that might otherwise be tough to digest. Warm food is ideal when you are tired or have a delicate gut because it requires much less energy to digest, leaving more for you to devote to the things you love doing.

From collagen-rich broths to probiotics that help restore your microbiome, these satisfying bowls of goodness will restore your equilibrium in the most delicious way. I like to have a cup of bone broth as a night cap when I'm feeling stressed, rather than a mug of cocoa; the magnesium content relaxes muscles for an untroubled night's sleep.

MINTY PEA AND WATERCRESS SOUP
WITH MILK KEFIR

Serves 4

With some frozen peas and good chicken broth, you can conjure up the summer in a matter of moments with this fresh, creamy soup. The green parts of spring onions are easier to digest than the white, so stick to these if you are sensitive. If you are not sensitive, for a more prebiotic meal, use the whole onion and add a few garlic cloves. Milk kefir is a fantastic source of lactic bacteria that help soothe an inflamed gut – use coconut kefir if you are sensitive to dairy.

2 heaped teaspoons salted butter

1 tablespoon olive oil

10 spring onions, roughly chopped

1 garlic clove, finely chopped (optional)

150g (5oz) watercress, roughly chopped

700g (1lb 9oz) frozen peas

500ml (18fl oz) chicken Bone Broth or Vegetable Broth (see pages 53–54)

Large handful of mint leaves, plus extra for decoration

Juice of ½–1 lemon

150ml (¼ pint) milk kefir (or live natural yoghurt)

Sea salt and freshly ground black pepper

Melt the butter and olive oil in a large pan over a medium heat, then add the spring onions and soften gently for 5 minutes or so. Add the garlic now if you are using it. Add the watercress to the pan when the onions are soft and sweet, cook for a couple of minutes, then add the frozen peas and broth and bring to the boil.

Half fill the sink with cold water and have a mixing bowl ready. As soon as the peas come back up to the boil and float, pour the contents of the pan into the mixing bowl and place this carefully in the cold water in the sink to cool a little.

Pour the pea mixture into a blender with the mint leaves, juice of ½ lemon and a few pinches of salt and a grind of black pepper. Whizz until velvety smooth and then taste to see if it needs more lemon juice, salt or pepper. You can eat this soup hot or at room temperature – cool is my preference. If you want to eat it hot, reheat gently, but don't let it boil.

Pour into bowls and stir in half of the milk kefir – about a heaped tablespoon per bowl. Swirl the remainder on top, grind a little extra black pepper over and top with some extra mint leaves.

ROAST TOMATO SOUP WITH CRÈME FRAÎCHE AND BEET KVASS

Serves 4

The secret to this creamy soup is to cook everything long and slow, so that every last morsel of sugar is coaxed out of the vegetables and the caramel tones of roasting come through. A candy pink mixture of crème fraîche and beet kvass provides a probiotic swirl atop the orange soup – it reminds me a little of those fruit salad chews I used to ruin my teeth with as a child. If you don't have beet kvass, try a little beet juice.

1 tablespoon chicken or duck fat

1.25kg (2¾lb) cherry tomatoes (or other sweet tomatoes)

3 tablespoons olive oil

2 courgettes, peeled and diced

Bunch of spring onions, roughly chopped (use only the green parts for low FODMAP)

1 large carrot, diced

1 celery stick, diced

300–400ml (10–14fl oz) Bone Broth (see page 53) or water

4 tablespoons crème fraîche

3 tablespoons Beet Kvass (see page 244)

Black Sesame Crumb (see page 215)

Sea salt and freshly ground black pepper

Preheat the oven to 200°C/180°C fan/gas 6. Divide the fat between two baking trays and warm in the oven for a few minutes, then add the cherry tomatoes, turning to coat. Roast for about 45 minutes, until the tomato skins are charred and the juices are starting to caramelise a little.

Meanwhile, heat the olive oil in a pan set over a low heat, add the courgettes, spring onions, carrot and celery and cook gently for at least 20 minutes, stirring occasionally, until soft and starting to caramelise.

Blend the roast tomatoes and softened vegetables with enough bone broth to make a smooth, thick soup. Season to taste with salt and pepper, reheat gently to serving temperature, then pour into bowls.

Mix the crème fraîche and beet kvass together to make a creamy, pink sauce and swirl a spoonful into each bowl. Sprinkle with sesame crumbs and put more of both on the table for people to help themselves.

NANA'S CHICKEN SOUP

Serves 4

My Nana was much more likely to open a tin of soup than cook from scratch, so this simple, soothing soup is something that I imagine other Nanas make when folks need a little gentle comfort and their tummies want only calming food to eat. Low in FODMAPs, it's a great thing to eat if you're having a stressful week and your stomach is in knots. Let Nana make it better.

2 heaped teaspoons chicken, duck or goose fat

4 chicken thighs (bone in, skin on)

3 large celery sticks, cut into 1cm (½in) dice

1 very large or 2 medium fennel bulbs, cut into 1cm (½in) dice

4 large carrots, cut into 1cm (½in) dice

500g (1lb 2oz) salad potatoes, diced

1 litre (1¾ pints) Bone Broth or Vegetable Broth (see pages 53–54)

2 bay leaves

2 courgettes, diced

8 spring onions, sliced

Sea salt and freshly ground black pepper

Heat half of the fat in a large pan, put the chicken thighs in, skin side down, brown for about 5 minutes and then remove and set aside. Keep the fat in the pan.

Add the celery, fennel and carrots to the pan, then sauté over a medium-low heat, allowing the vegetables to soften and sweeten, stirring often, for about 20 minutes. Towards the end of this time they should start to take a little colour as the sugars caramelise. When you're starting to challenge your gut a little more, add a leek, onion or even some garlic to the soup at this stage.

Add the potatoes to the pan with the broth, bay leaves and chicken thighs. Cover the pan and simmer gently for 45 minutes.

Take the chicken out of the pan and as soon as it is cool enough, pull the skin off and set aside. Put the chicken thighs back into the pan with the courgettes, season well and simmer for another 10 minutes.

Meanwhile, in a separate pan, gently fry the chicken skin in the remaining fat until it is golden brown on both sides. Drain on kitchen paper and sprinkle with a little salt. Add the spring onions to the soup (only the green parts for low FODMAP) and fish out the bay leaves.

Ladle the soup into bowls, shred the chicken meat over it (discard the bones) and top each portion with a piece of crispy chicken skin. The parsley dressing from Green Potato Salad (see page 157) is delicious drizzled over the top.

BONE BROTH

Serves 4

Connective tissues contain the amino acid glutamine that helps to close up the tight junctions in the gut lining, and bones contain easily absorbed minerals, such as calcium and magnesium. Bone broth can be drunk like tea, with a spoonful of miso, or used for soups and stews that will repair and restore. Save any bones that you have left after a meal and freeze until you have enough for a pot of broth. Butchers will often give away marrow bones and chicken carcasses for next to nothing.

1 or 2 chicken carcasses or the equivalent in beef, pork or lamb bones – or the bones left from any kind of roast (include any giblets, skin or bits that you haven't eaten)

1 celery stick, chopped

1 carrot, chopped

2 bay leaves (rosemary or thyme for lamb broth)

5 black peppercorns

If your carcasses/bones are raw, preheat the oven to 200°C/180°C fan/gas 6 and roast them in a roasting tin for about 30–40 minutes, until the skin and meat is starting to take on a lovely golden colour and smell deliciously roasty. Bones from a roast dinner can be used as they are – don't worry about germs as they won't survive the long simmer.

Put the bones, giblets, celery, carrot, bay leaves and peppercorns in a lidded pan large enough to take everything and leave a decent space on top. Cover everything with water and bring to the boil. Reduce the heat to a trembling simmer, cover with a tight-fitting lid and cook for 6–24 hours, topping up with water if necessary, so that the bones are always covered. I tend to make my broth after supper, let it simmer all evening, leave it to cool slowly overnight and then give it a few hours the next morning. If you can't boil it again until the next evening, put it in the fridge for the day and complete the broth in the evening. A slow cooker is brilliant for this. Don't undercook it or the gelatine and minerals won't leach out.

When it's done, strain through a sieve into a large bowl and discard the bones, etc. I then strain it straight into clean glass jars, put a lid on and chill in the fridge once cool, before freezing. Tupperware, freezer bags or ice cube trays are alternatives to jars for freezing. This bone broth keeps for up to 5 days in the fridge or up to 3 months in the freezer.

When I defrost the broth, if I don't want to use the fat on top, I just scoop it into a little jar and keep it in the fridge. You can also cool the broth in a large bowl and scrape off the fat before you put it into jars – it's tasty and good for you so don't throw it away, whatever you do.

FISH BROTH

Thought to be an excellent tonic for the thyroid and a source of particularly joint-friendly collagen and minerals, fish broth also contains beneficial fats and antioxidant, astaxanthin, to help calm inflammation. Follow the guidelines on page 53, substituting raw or cooked fish bones and heads for the meat and 1 teaspoon fennel seeds for the bay leaves. Don't use oily fish for this and if you are using fish spines, remove the bloodline (darker flesh) down the centre with a sharp knife. Fish broth only needs to be cooked for about an hour (2 hours max) until it tastes delicious, and it is best to skim off any scum that rises, as this can be bitter. You can also add a glass of white wine or sake for a little acidity that balances the fish beautifully. Strain and proceed as for Bone Broth on page 53. This broth keeps for up to 3 days in the fridge or up to a month in the freezer.

VEGETABLE BROTH

Vegetable peelings, dried or fresh mushrooms and seaweed all make delicious vegetable broths. They don't have the gelatine contained in meat and fish broths, but they are mineral-rich and quick to make. Save the ends of leeks, onions, bits of celery you won't eat, knobbly bits of celeriac (washed first), squash peel, potato peelings – in fact everything except turnip, radish, swede and all members of the cabbage family. If you have some dried mushrooms, then a tablespoon of these will go a long way, but a few chopped fresh button mushrooms will help too. Freeze the vegetables if you don't gather enough in a week. Add a couple of carrots, 1 whole onion (skin on) and at least 1 celery stick to your mix of peelings.

Dice the carrots, onion and celery and sauté very gently in 1 tablespoon of butter, olive oil or coconut oil for about 20 minutes, until they are soft and sweet smelling. Add all the peelings, mushrooms, etc, a bay leaf, a sprig of thyme and a curl of orange rind or 1 teaspoon of fennel seeds, if you like. Cover everything with water, bring to the boil and simmer for up to an hour, skimming off any scum that rises. You can add a 10cm piece of kambu seaweed to the broth after it has come off the heat. Leave for 10 minutes, strain and proceed as for Bone Broth on page 53. This broth keeps for up to 5 days in the fridge or up to 3 months in the freezer.

MISO SOUP WITH RIBBON PICKLE

Serves 2

Miso is a fermented bean paste usually made from soya beans and often rice or barley, too. A living fermented food and beneficial form of soya, it has a deeply savoury flavour, full of umami and small amounts of glutamine that help repair the gut lining. I make my miso soup with bone broth or vegetable broth, rather than the more traditional dashi made with kombu (kelp) and bonito flakes, but I do add kombu as it also contains glutamine. In colder months, miso soup makes a perfect starter for sluggish digestion. If your gut needs a little TLC, leave the bits out and drink the broth through the day to calm inflammation.

2 garlic cloves, roughly chopped

4 spring onions, sliced (reserving a few green bits for garnish)

700ml (1¼ pints) Bone Broth, Fish Broth or Vegetable Broth (see pages 53–54)

100g (4oz) silken tofu, diced

10cm (4in) strip of dried kombu (kelp) seaweed, cut into a few pieces

2 teaspoons miso paste (red or genmai is my favourite)

Ribbon Pickle (see page 209)

Dried green nori flakes (optional)

Put the garlic and spring onions into a pan with the broth, then bring to the boil, cover and simmer for 15 minutes. Strain out the bits, return the broth to the pan and bring back to a simmer.

Add the tofu to the broth and simmer for 5 minutes, then turn off the heat. Stir in the kombu (don't wash it beforehand as the white powder contains glutamine), cover and leave for 10 minutes.

Remove the kombu and discard, or refrigerate it in an airtight container for up to 3 days and use once more for another batch of soup. Put the miso paste in a little bowl and loosen it with some of the broth, then gradually pour this into the pan, tasting as you go. Remember that the ribbon pickle will be a little salty, so don't make it quite as salty as you would like it to end up.

Ladle the soup into a couple of bowls, top each with a tangle of ribbon pickle (about 30–40g/1¼–1½oz per serving), a sprinkle of nori flakes and the reserved spring onion tops. The soup should be at the right temperature to eat – try to avoid heating it up if you can, or do so very gently.

SALADS & VEGETABLES

BUCKWHEAT AND AVOCADO SALAD WITH FENNEL AND WILD ROSE

GINGHAM SALAD

SWEET CARROTS AND SAVOURY CHARD

GRIDDLED COURGETTES WITH SALSA VERDE

PAPAYA, CUCUMBER AND LIME SALAD WITH CORIANDER LEAF

FRESH FIGS WITH WATERCRESS AND GOATS' MILK LABNEH

VELVETY CARROT PURÉE

AUBERGINE SLIPPERS WITH CORIANDER YOGHURT AND BLACK SESAME CRUMB

FRENCH PEAS AND GEM LETTUCE

FENNEL AND LEMON CARPACCIO

Vegetables are the vibrant, colourful heart of a healthy diet and yet so many of them can be tough to digest if you have a sensitive gut. This chapter makes the most of vegetables and fruit that are easier to digest and brings them to life with piquant dressings, herbs and crunchy sprinkles.

If you have a garden, you can plant the vegetables that you know your tummy will love; a small patch of courgettes can produce jars of pickles, plates of salad and courgette caviar on hand for breakfasts through the summer. Even if you don't have any ground to call your own, grow herbs on your windowsill to bring flavour to all your meals.

Start by peeling vegetables if you find them too fibrous and then gradually include more roughage in your diet as your gut becomes stronger.

BUCKWHEAT AND AVOCADO SALAD WITH FENNEL AND WILD ROSE

Serves 4

Said to soothe anxiety and balance hormones, fresh rose has a fruity fragrance that complements buckwheat perfectly. Fennel and lemon balm are similarly soothing and uplifting – definitely worth finding space for in your garden. If you can't find fennel herb, then a thinly shaved fennel bulb will do, and all garden rose petals are edible – just ask before you pinch some from the neighbours! Soaking garlic in oil imparts the flavour without the FODMAPs.

3 garlic cloves, finely chopped

100ml (3½fl oz) olive oil

240g (9oz) buckwheat groats

Juice of 1 lemon

½ teaspoon Dijon mustard

2 pinches of sea salt, or to taste

4 ripe avocados

2 handfuls of lemon balm leaves

30–40 herb fennel fronds (or 1 fennel bulb, shaved thinly using a mandolin)

Petals from 12 wild roses (or small garden roses)

Flaked sea salt, to finish

Put the garlic into a small bowl with the olive oil and leave to steep for 2–12 hours (the garlic flavour will become stronger the longer you leave it). Strain out the bits through a tea strainer and reserve the oil.

Put the buckwheat groats into a dry frying pan or large saucepan and toast over a medium heat, stirring constantly, until they are slightly darker in colour and smell nutty, about 10 minutes.

Pour 600ml (1 pint) water into the pan, bring to the boil and cover with a lid. Turn the heat down and simmer for 10–15 minutes, until all the water is absorbed. Check by parting the grains to see the bottom of the pan. Take off the heat, leave the lid on for 5 more minutes to steam and then tip out onto a plate to cool completely.

Make the dressing in a small, lidded jar using the lemon juice, reserved garlic oil, mustard and salt. Shake vigorously to emulsify and taste for seasoning.

Moisten the buckwheat with a little of the dressing and divide evenly between four dinner plates. Halve and remove the stones from the avocados, then using a teaspoon, scoop out large chunks of flesh and arrange these over the buckwheat.

Scatter lemon balm leaves over and lay fennel fronds around. Finally, scatter with rose petals (don't wash) and then drizzle the remaining dressing over with a teaspoon. Scatter with a little flaked sea salt, to finish.

GINGHAM SALAD

Serves 4

Reminiscent of the pink and white checks of a gingham tablecloth, this creamy potato salad says summer barbecue to me. Cold potatoes are a great source of resistant starch, so this is a great thing to have in the fridge for easy lunches. Commercial mayonnaise is inflammatory due to the damaged fats it contains, so I use rich, probiotic crème fraîche instead. If you can digest onions, add a handful of sliced spring onions or blanched red onion slivers.

300g (11oz) pink radishes

600g (1lb 5oz) waxy salad potatoes, boiled, then cooled and chilled for at least 3 hours

Bunch of chives, finely snipped

6 heaped tablespoons full-fat crème fraîche (about 175g/6oz)

2 pinches of sea salt

Freshly ground black pepper

Leave a little green tuft at the top if your radishes have their leaves, and slice into quarters. Put into a mixing bowl, reserving a few pretty ones for the top.

Cut the potatoes into pieces that are a similar size to the quartered radishes and add to the bowl. Reserve a teaspoonful of chives and add the remainder to the bowl.

In a small bowl, mix the crème fraîche with 2–3 tablespoons water, the salt and lots of black pepper, until it has the consistency of a loose mayonnaise.

Stir the dressing into the potato mixture until coated, check for seasoning and then scatter the top with the reserved chives and radishes, plus more black pepper.

SWEET CARROTS AND SAVOURY CHARD

Serves 4

Chard is much easier to digest than cabbage and yet it has all those wonderful dark green nutrients and plenty of fibre too. The earthy flavour of chard is wonderful with salty miso and the contrast of carrots cooked quickly so they caramelise a little at the edges. Miso is rich with good bacteria, while honey contains enzymes, and both are damaged by heat, so these are added after cooking.

300g (11oz) Swiss chard, washed

2 tablespoons duck, chicken or bacon fat

4 carrots, cut into matchsticks

Pinch of sea salt

1 tablespoon genmai miso

1 tablespoon finely grated fresh root ginger

2 teaspoons raw honey

Good handful of Spicy Pumpkin Seeds (see page 220)

Chop off the chard stalks where they meet the leaf and cut into the same lengths as the carrot matchsticks. Roughly chop the chard leaves and set aside. Heat 1 tablespoon of the fat in a wok or large frying pan and add the carrots, chard stalks and salt. Cook over a high heat, shaking the pan frequently, but allowing the carrots to catch a little and caramelise. When they are al dente and a little charred at the edges, tip into a bowl, cover and return the wok to the stove.

Mix the miso with 1 tablespoon of water in a mixing bowl and set aside. Heat the remaining fat in the wok, add the chard leaves and ginger and stir-fry over a high heat, until the leaves have wilted. Tip into the miso mixture and turn to coat.

Mix the honey into the carrots and chard stalks. Spread the stir-fried chard leaves out on a serving plate, top with a tangle of carrots and chard stalks, then sprinkle a good handful of spicy pumpkin seeds over the top.

I like to eat this with some fried tempeh seasoned with tamari and chilli (see the Ramen Bowl recipe on page 166), cherry tomatoes, steamed rice and Tahini Sauce (see page 224).

GRIDDLED COURGETTES WITH SALSA VERDE

Serves 4

Griddling brings a smoky sweetness to the courgettes, and piquant salsa verde makes this salad a great accompaniment for roast meat, fish or even a plate of scrambled eggs. Herbs are packed with minerals and antioxidants, and the sharp saltiness of salsa verde stimulates the digestive process, so it's worth making extra sauce to add to other meals (it keeps well for up to 5 days in an airtight jar in the fridge).

3 courgettes, trimmed

Small bunch of flat-leaf parsley

½ bunch of mint

Small bunch of basil

1 tablespoon salted capers, well-rinsed

2 tinned anchovies, drained

1 teaspoon Dijon mustard

2–3 teaspoons red wine vinegar

100ml (3½fl oz) Garlic Oil (see page 225)

Freshly ground black pepper

Peel the courgettes into long, wide strips with a vegetable peeler. Put a dry griddle pan over a high heat and griddle the strips on one side, one layer at a time, until you can see the char marks coming through on the edges. Use tongs to transfer the cooked courgettes to a mixing bowl and repeat with another layer of strips. If you don't have a griddle pan, try cooking the strips under a really hot grill, just until they wilt – you won't have the char marks or flavour though.

To make the salsa verde, pick the leaves from the parsley, mint and basil and put into a blender with the capers, anchovies, mustard, wine vinegar, three-quarters of the garlic oil and lots of black pepper. Blend in bursts, scraping down, until you have a coarse, loose paste. Add more garlic oil or vinegar if you think it needs it.

Alternatively, chop everything very finely on a board and then mix with the vinegar and garlic oil in a bowl or using a pestle and mortar.

Combine the salsa verde with the griddled courgettes while still warm, and serve immediately.

PAPAYA, CUCUMBER AND LIME SALAD
WITH CORIANDER LEAF

Serves 4

Soft, mild papaya really comes alive when you introduce it to sharp lime and fragrant coriander. Papaya is both richly antioxidant and helps with digestion of protein due to the enzymes it contains, making this salad a great companion for meat, fish or cheese. If your tummy likes heat, some finely chopped fresh chilli sets off all those cool clean flavours nicely.

2 cucumbers

2 ripe papayas, peeled, halved and seeds scooped out

4 spring onions or ½ red onion

2 large handfuls of coriander leaves

2 tablespoons black sesame seeds

Juice of 2 juicy limes

3–4 teaspoons raw honey

3–4 pinches of sea salt

Using a vegetable peeler, shave each cucumber into long strips (seeds and all) and put into a mixing bowl. Slice the papaya flesh into half moons and add to the cucumber.

If you are sensitive to FODMAPs, just slice the green parts of the spring onions, and if not, slice the white parts too, or use the red onion, finely sliced. Add the onions to the bowl with most of the coriander leaves, reserving a few for decoration.

Toast the sesame seeds in a dry pan over a medium heat for a few minutes, shaking the pan constantly, until they start popping and smell toasty. Set aside to cool.

In a small bowl, mix the lime juice with the honey and salt, check for seasoning and then pour over the salad, turning gently with your hands.

Arrange the salad on four plates and scatter with the reserved coriander leaves and the toasted sesame seeds. Eat immediately before the papaya softens and the lime oxidises.

FRESH FIGS WITH WATERCRESS AND GOATS' MILK LABNEH

Serves 4

Goats' milk labneh has some of the sourness of goats' cheese but none of the pungency, making it a perfect partner for fresh figs. The peppery bite of watercress and bitterness of toasted walnuts and buckwheat make this salad a wonderfully balanced dish that also happens to contain omega-3 fats, calcium and acidophilus in abundance. If you see some great fresh figs, snap them up and make this immediately, because just like a great pear, they don't stay that way for long.

100g (4oz) walnuts

80g (3oz) watercress leaves

4 ripe fresh figs

200g (7oz) Goats' Milk Labneh (see page 210)

1 x quantity of Velvet Dressing recipe (see page 226)

1–2 tablespoons date syrup

1 tablespoon toasted buckwheat groats (see Buckwheat Tea recipe on page 235)

Set a dry frying pan over a high heat, add the walnuts and toast until they start to catch on the tips. Set aside to cool.

Divide the watercress between four plates (or one large platter), discarding any woody stalks. Slice the figs and scatter these over the watercress, then dot pieces of labneh around the figs. Break the walnuts up a little in your hands and scatter these over, too.

Drizzle velvet dressing over the whole thing just before you eat and do Jackson Pollock-style artistry with the date syrup too. Scatter with the toasted buckwheat and serve immediately.

For a more substantial supper, this salad is delicious with a little pink roast lamb and some steamed French beans on the side.

VELVETY CARROT PURÉE

Serves 4

A healthy dose of fresh turmeric root makes this carrot purée as orange as a hi-vis jacket – something that brings me immense joy! Rich, garlicky and fragrant, it is equally delicious cold for dipping veg sticks or hunks of bread into, or served warm alongside slices of pink lamb and dark greens.

75ml (3fl oz) olive oil

2 garlic cloves, finely sliced

5 large carrots, peeled or scrubbed and chopped into rough chunks

2 teaspoons light tahini

Thumb-sized piece of fresh turmeric root, peeled and grated

½ teaspoon ground cumin

Finely grated zest of ¼ lemon, plus juice of ½ lemon (or to taste)

Sea salt

Put the olive oil and garlic into a small bowl and leave to infuse for at least an hour, before straining off and discarding the garlic pieces (steeping garlic in oil this way gives you the flavour without the FODMAPs). Reserve the oil.

Put the carrots into a lidded saucepan with 100ml (3½fl oz) of water, cover, bring to a gentle boil, then simmer for 15–20 minutes, until the water is absorbed and the carrots are soft. Top up with a splash of water if necessary, or leave the lid off to evaporate any water that is not absorbed.

Set the carrots aside to cool a little and then tip into a food-processor with the tahini, turmeric, garlicky olive oil, ground cumin and the lemon zest and juice. Whizz until the mixture starts to become smoother and then season with a few pinches of salt.

Now taste and decide if you need more lemon juice or salt and purée until the mixture is velvety smooth. If the mixture seems stiff, add some more olive oil and a little water to loosen it up, and whizz again.

AUBERGINE SLIPPERS WITH CORIANDER YOGHURT AND BLACK SESAME CRUMB

Serves 4

A roast aubergine is about as meaty and satisfying as a vegetable can get — sweetly caramelised about the edges with rich yielding flesh. Paired with a creamy, fragrant dressing and toasty sesame crumbs, it could easily be a main course with a simple salad on the side — double the quantities if you do this. Marinating garlic in oil allows you to enjoy the flavour without the consequences for a more delicate gut. As your digestion improves, try making a paste with a little of the garlic and adding this to the aubergine, increasing the amount as you tolerate more.

2 large aubergines

100ml (3½fl oz) Garlic Oil (see page 225)

A little sea salt

30g (1¼oz) coriander leaves

125g (4½oz) live natural yoghurt

Juice of 1 lemon, or to taste

½ x quantity of Black Sesame Crumb recipe (see page 215), to serve

Preheat the oven to 180°C/160°C fan/gas 4. Slice each aubergine in half lengthways through the stalk and then score the flesh into diamonds with a knife, taking care not to puncture the skin. Place, cut side up, on a baking sheet, drizzle the garlic oil evenly over the aubergine flesh, then sprinkle with a little salt. Roast for about an hour, until the flesh is soft and deeply golden on top.

While the aubergines roast, make the coriander yoghurt. Put the coriander leaves, yoghurt and a good squeeze of lemon juice into a blender and whizz until the sauce is a pale green colour. Taste for lemon and add a little more if necessary, then pour into a little bowl and set aside.

To serve, give everyone an aubergine slipper and let them help themselves to the coriander yoghurt and sesame crumb.

FRENCH PEAS AND GEM LETTUCE

Serves 4

Cooking Little Gem lettuce really brings out a sweet, buttery quality that makes humble frozen peas taste as though they are freshly plucked from a summer garden. If your digestion is sluggish, cooked vegetables are much easier to digest than a big plate of salad. Bone broth and butter make this a gut-soothing side for any number of meals. Add some sliced spring onions with the peas as your gut health improves.

400ml (14fl oz) chicken Bone Broth (see page 53)

4 rashers streaky bacon

4 Little Gem lettuces, washed

2 teaspoons salted butter

500g (1lb 2oz) frozen peas

Sea salt and freshly ground black pepper

Bring the bone broth to the boil in a small pan. Meanwhile, fry the bacon rashers in a frying pan over a medium heat, until crisp all over, then set aside to cool.

Cut the lettuces in half along their length. Melt the butter in a large lidded pan that will hold all the lettuce halves in one layer (or cook them in batches in a smaller pan). Brown the lettuce halves over a medium heat ensuring you don't burn the butter.

Add the peas and hot broth to the pan and bring back to the boil, cooking for just a few minutes, until the peas are completely defrosted.

Strain the veg through a colander, catching the juices in a bowl beneath. Return the juices to the pan and cook over a high heat for a few minutes to reduce them to a syrupy consistency.

Return the veg to the pan, turn to coat, check for salt and serve with lots of black pepper and the bacon rashers crumbled over the top.

FENNEL AND LEMON CARPACCIO

Serves 4

The sweetness of fennel is a perfect partner for bitter, sharp lemon slices in this piquant salad. It makes a great starter or accompaniment to rich food, as the lemon stimulates the salivary glands and supports the liver, ensuring your meal is better digested. It is much easier to make with a mandolin, but you can use a vegetable peeler to shave everything into wafer thin slices.

1 fennel bulb

1 juicy lemon (Cedro, if you can find them)

Olive oil (or cold-pressed sunflower oil)

½ teaspoon Dijon mustard

Raw honey (optional)

Couple of pinches of sea salt

Good grind of black pepper

100g (4oz) Labneh (see page 210)

Fennel Seed Dukkah (see page 218)

1 head of fennel flowers or chive flowers (optional)

Shave the fennel bulb using a mandolin or vegetable peeler and spread onto a serving plate. Shave half of the lemon into wafer thin slices and cover the fennel with these.

Juice the remaining half of the lemon and pour into a lidded jar with twice the amount of olive oil, mustard and a little honey (if using), then shake together to emulsify.

Drizzle the dressing over the fennel and lemon, then scatter with the salt and pepper. Tear off pieces of the labneh and dip into the dukkah, then dot over the salad. Finally, scatter with fennel or chive flowers if you have them and serve immediately.

MEALS

CORIANDER MEATBALLS WITH LEMON-SPIKED YOGHURT

GINGERY FISH PARCELS

SALT COD CROQUETAS

LEMONY FETA BURGERS AND A HEAP OF BUTTERY GREENS

ROAST FISH ON A BED OF VEGETABLES

LICK-YOUR-FINGERS CHICKEN

PEA AND BASIL TART WITH A BUTTERY OAT CRUST

BUTTERY SCALLOPS WITH CREAMY AND CRISPY PARSNIPS AND A LUSCIOUS SALAD

BLACK RICE NOODLE BOWL

Every meal should feel like an opportunity to settle down and nourish yourself joyfully, but it's easy to get overwhelmed by decisions about what to cook when you can't eat certain things. Rather than focusing on what you can't have, these meals celebrate all the wonderful, buttery, finger-licking food that you will want to eat, whether your tummy is delicate or not.

I like to make one meal for everyone that accounts for different tastes and tolerances but doesn't feel like a free-from compromise. Preserved lemons, gingery pickles and smoked paprika bring the oomph to these meals that is lacking in so many restricted diets, while labneh and miso are full of umami that makes food so savoury and delicious.

CORIANDER MEATBALLS WITH LEMON-SPIKED YOGHURT

Serves 4

This is one of those easy meals that makes you thankful you took a little time at the weekend to make some dukkah and a jar of ribbon pickle. Anti-inflammatory coriander leaf works well against sweet parsnip, while the gingery pickle and lemon-spiked yoghurt provide a tart probiotic contrast. Sprinkle some spicy dukkah on top and I can guarantee that your taste buds will be tickled right to the end of supper.

FOR THE PARSNIP MASH

800g (1¾lb) parsnips, peeled and cut into rough chunks

Generous glug of cold-pressed rapeseed oil or cold-pressed sunflower oil (or 25g/1oz butter)

Fresh lemon juice, to taste

Sea salt and freshly ground black pepper

FOR THE CORIANDER MEATBALLS

4 spring onions

75g (3oz) coriander leaves (a medium bunch), finely chopped

400g (14oz) pork mince

3 pinches of sea salt

Few teaspoons duck or goose fat, lard or dripping, for frying

TO SERVE

300g (11oz) live natural yoghurt

1½ tablespoons chopped Preserved Lemon (see page 203)

Juice of 1 lemon, or to taste

100g (4oz) watercress

Ribbon Pickle (see page 209)

Dukkah (see page 218)

For the parsnip mash, steam the parsnips until very tender, about 10-15 minutes, then drain and mash. For a very fine purée, push the parsnips through a sieve into a mixing bowl using a wooden spoon and a scraping motion, or use a potato masher for something much chunkier. I find that a blender makes parsnip purée very gloopy, so I don't use one. Pour in a generous glug of oil (or use salted butter), a few pinches of sea salt and lots of black pepper and then point up the flavour with some lemon juice. Thin with a little boiling water if need be. Keep warm and warm the plates too.

For the meatballs, finely chop the green part of the spring onions (or the whole thing if you can tolerate it). Put into a mixing bowl with the coriander, pork mince and salt, mixing together well with your hands. Form the mixture into 20 balls and set aside briefly.

Mix the yoghurt, preserved lemon and enough lemon juice to make a zingy yoghurt dressing, thinning it with a little water if it is very thick – it should be the texture of thick double cream.

Heat the fat in a frying pan and gently fry the meatballs until they are golden all over and cooked through but still succulent, about 6–8 minutes.

To serve, spread the parsnip mash on one side of each plate, drizzle half of the yoghurt sauce over it and top with the meatballs. Put the watercress on the other side of the plates, add a tangle of ribbon pickle and then scatter dukkah over the whole thing. Put the remaining yoghurt sauce, plus more ribbon pickle and dukkah on the table for people to help themselves.

GINGERY FISH PARCELS

Serves 4

Baking in foil seals in the flavour, keeps fish succulent and lends an enjoyably Blue Peter-ish element to supper. When you open your steamy parcel at the table, the scent of sweet arame seaweed, warming ginger and fragrant lemon zest is mouth-watering! You can make and chill the parcels in the fridge (before cooking) up to 24 hours in advance, if you need to.

35g (1¼oz) dried arame seaweed

700g (1lb 9oz) sustainable salmon fillet (skin on) or 4 mackerel fillets (skin on)

Finely grated zest of 1 lemon, plus 4 teaspoons fresh lemon juice

1 tablespoon peeled and finely grated fresh root ginger

4 teaspoons genmai miso

4 large spring onions, sliced (use the green parts only if you are sensitive to FODMAPs)

Preheat the oven to 220°C/200°C fan/gas 7. Soak the arame seaweed in cool water for 15 minutes to rehydrate, then drain and rinse well. Slice the salmon fillet into 4 equal pieces. In a small bowl, mix together the lemon zest, lemon juice, grated ginger and miso.

Cut four 30cm (12in) lengths of foil and four 20cm (8in) square pieces of baking parchment. Lay out the foil with a square of parchment in the centre of each piece.

Place a little pile of arame in the centre of each parchment square, top with the spring onions and then a portion of fish. Spread the miso mixture equally along the top of each fish portion.

Seal up each parcel by bringing together the edges of the foil above the fish and fold over a few times to seal the seam. Squash either end down a little and turn this over too, to seal the entire package.

Bake for 12–15 minutes, depending on the thickness of your fish portions, until the fish is just opaque and flakes easily. Serve with steamed greens, boiled rice and Tahini Sauce (see page 224).

SALT COD CROQUETAS

Serves 4

Fish was traditionally salted to preserve it for lean times when nothing fresh could be caught, and it is generally as salty as an olive. Now we have fridges and freezers, I like to salt fish lightly to draw out some of the water and firm up the texture, making it perfect for making these delicious croquetas that are crisp and nutty outside and soft inside. They work brilliantly with frozen fish, can be made well in advance and are an incredibly moreish way of making fish go further.

300g (11oz) sustainable skinless cod fillet or other sustainable white fish

2 teaspoons sea salt

600ml (1 pint) milk or milk alternative

2 bay leaves

300g (11oz) floury potatoes, peeled and quartered

Bunch of chives, finely snipped

Large handful of flat-leaf parsley, finely chopped

2 heaped teaspoons flour (buckwheat, teff, oat or rye)

250g (9oz) lard or dripping

Sea salt and freshly ground black pepper

TO SERVE

250g (9oz) French beans, trimmed (or leftover roast vegetables)

1 x Velvet Dressing recipe (see page 226)

1 romaine or cos lettuce or 2 Little Gem lettuces, washed and patted dry

100g (4oz) watercress

Handful of radishes, sliced or quartered

Handful of Spicy Pumpkin Seeds (see page 220)

8–24 hours before you plan to make these, rub the fish with the salt, place on a plate, cover with clingfilm or an upturned plate and chill in the fridge.

Wash the salted fish in cold water and place into a wide pan with the milk and bay leaves, bring gently to the boil, then simmer for about 4–5 minutes, until the fish flakes easily. Lift the fish out of the milk and put into a bowl. Discard the bay leaves. Add the potatoes to the same milk and cook until soft, about 15 minutes, then drain and discard the milk.

Check there are no bones in the fish and mash it with a fork until completely shredded. Mash the potatoes and add them to the fish along with the chives, parsley and flour. Mix well and add lots of black pepper and a little salt if needed.

Either roll the croquetas between your palms or shape them between two dessertspoons into an oval; you should make about 16. Keep a teaspoonful back to test the frying temperature. You can now chill the croquetas in the fridge for up to 24 hours, or even freeze them for up to a month (defrost them in the fridge for a few hours before frying).

To make the salad for serving, steam the French beans for about 4–5 minutes, refresh briefly under cold water, then drain and tip into a mixing bowl with the velvet dressing. Tear the lettuce leaves into rough pieces and add to the bowl with the watercress and radishes. Toss everything together just before you are about to eat and scatter with the spicy pumpkin seeds.

Heat the lard or dripping for shallow-frying and when it is hot but not smoking, add your reserved teaspoon of croqueta mixture. It should turn deep golden brown in about a minute. Fry the croquetas in batches, until they are golden brown all over, about 3–4 minutes per batch. Drain on kitchen paper and serve immediately. Some Probiotic Ketchup (see page 228) or Tahini Sauce (see page 224) is a delicious accompaniment, too.

LEMONY FETA BURGERS AND A HEAP OF BUTTERY GREENS

Serves 4

These fresh summery burgers are quick to make and packed with flavour. Lemon zest has excellent antioxidant qualities that help prevent cell damage, and it really sings with mint and tangy feta cheese. You can make the burgers up to 24 hours in advance (keep them in the fridge), or even freeze them for easy workday meals.

FOR THE LEMONY FETA BURGERS

200g (7oz) frozen peas

200g (7oz) feta cheese

Large bunch of chives, finely snipped

Large handful of mint leaves, finely chopped

100g (4oz) fresh sourdough breadcrumbs, plus extra for coating

Finely grated zest of 1½ lemons

1½ tablespoons flour (buckwheat, rye or teff), plus extra for dusting

1 organic egg

250g (9oz) lard or dripping, for shallow-frying

FOR THE HEAP OF BUTTERY GREENS

300g (11oz) French beans, trimmed

200g (7oz) frozen peas

50g (2oz) salted butter

450g (1lb) spinach leaves (large ones if possible), washed and patted dry

1 teaspoon sherry vinegar (or other vinegar)

Sea salt and freshly ground black pepper

TO SERVE

Spicy Pumpkin Seeds (see page 220)

Migas (see page 215)

For the burgers, bring some water to the boil in a small pan, add the peas and when they rise to the top, refresh with cold water, drain well, put into a mixing bowl and crush with a potato masher. Crumble the feta into the bowl, then add the chives, mint, breadcrumbs, lemon zest and flour. Squidge the mixture together with your hands, reserve a teaspoon of the mixture and then form the remainder into eight patties.

Beat the egg in a small bowl, put some extra flour in another small bowl and breadcrumbs in a third bowl. Dip each patty first into the flour, then the egg and finally the breadcrumbs, then set aside until you are ready to fry them.

For the greens, steam the French beans until just al dente, about 4 minutes, adding the peas after a minute. Refresh in cold water and drain well.

Heat the fat for shallow-frying the patties and test the heat by frying the reserved teaspoon of mixture first – it should brown in about a minute. Add the patties to the pan and fry until golden underneath, then turn and cook the other side until golden, about 6–7 minutes in total. Drain on kitchen paper while you finish the greens.

Gently melt the butter in a large saucepan or wok and when it starts to froth, add the spinach. Cook over a medium heat for a minute, just until it starts to wilt, then stir in the French beans, peas and vinegar. Season with salt and pepper and heat through.

Tip the greens onto a serving dish, scatter with spicy pumpkin seeds and migas and fold through briefly, then eat with the burgers.

ROAST FISH ON A BED OF VEGETABLES

Serves 4

I love a meal that can be assembled in a roasting tin and then emerge later, to fill the kitchen with deliciousness. Whole roast fish are surprisingly easy to serve as the flesh just lifts off the bones. This is a homely meal where nobody should stand on ceremony, so I tend to put everything on the table and let people help themselves. The vegetables are all easy to digest, but leave out the onions, or just avoid them if you are sensitive.

750g (1lb 10oz) salad potatoes

Olive oil, for drizzling

2 large fennel bulbs, each cut into 8 wedges

2 red onions, each cut into 8 wedges

400g (14oz) cherry vine tomatoes

1.2kg (2¾lb) whole flat fish (dab or brill) or mackerel or 4 large fresh sardines, gutted and descaled (ask your fishmonger to do this, if you prefer)

Lemon wedges

20g (¾oz) dill fronds

Sea salt

Cook the potatoes in a pan of boiling water until they are just tender to the point of a knife, about 10–15 minutes (or you can use previously cooked potatoes). Drain well and set aside until cool enough to handle. Preheat the oven to 180°C/160°C fan/gas 4.

Drizzle some olive oil onto two roasting trays, slice the potatoes into thick slabs and place in a single layer on the trays. Nestle the fennel and red onion wedges in among the potatoes. Drizzle everything generously with olive oil and sprinkle with salt, then roast for 45 minutes, basting the vegetables with the oil halfway through cooking.

Place the cherry tomatoes, still on their vines, around the edge of the trays, baste again and roast for another 15 minutes. Place the fish on top of the vegetables, baste with oil, sprinkle with salt and roast for about 15 minutes for sardines, 18–20 minutes for mackerel, or 25 minutes for dab or brill. The fish flesh should come away from the bone when you test it and be just opaque, but still soft and moist.

When the fish is done, put the lemon wedges around the fish and scatter dill fronds over both trays. Bring the trays to the table and let everyone help themselves.

VARIATION

This also works well with chicken thighs. After the veg have roasted for 45 minutes, place a chicken thigh per person on top of the vegetables and add the tomatoes to the trays. Roast for another 45–60 minutes, until the meat is cooked through and the skin is crisp.

LICK-YOUR-FINGERS CHICKEN

Serves 4

These days many people choose chicken breast over the dark meat and wouldn't dream of eating the skin or gnawing on the sticky delicious bits at the ends of the bones. Well I urge you to do just that; cook your meat on the bone, eat the skin and nibble on the cartilage that has grown soft during cooking. The amino acids they contain help you to break down the muscle protein, repair the gut mucosa and keep your skin plump. Rich, sticky, salty and lemony – I defy you not to lick your fingers when you eat these chicken thighs.

1 teaspoon chicken, duck or goose fat

4 chicken thighs (or a jointed chicken minus breasts)

4 bay leaves

1–2 Preserved Lemons (see page 203)

Freshly ground black pepper

Heat the fat in an ovenproof frying pan and then add the chicken thighs, skin side down. Fry for a few minutes, until the skin is lightly golden, then turn the thighs skin-side up, placing a bay leaf under each one as you do so. Add 50ml (2fl oz) of water to the pan, cover tightly with a lid and simmer over a low heat for 45 minutes. Check occasionally that the water hasn't completely evaporated and top up with a splash if it has.

Meanwhile, preheat the oven to 220°C/200°C fan/gas 7 (a conventional oven with top and bottom heat is best for crisping up the chicken skin). Scrape the flesh out of your preserved lemons and discard, then chop the rind finely. You will need about 4 heaped teaspoons of chopped lemon rind.

When the chicken has finished braising, spread the preserved lemon rind over the chicken skin and baste generously with the fat in the pan. Add a splash more water if the juices are starting to caramelise, just so they don't burn. Bake for 15 minutes, until the chicken skin is crisp around the edges and the lemon rind is caramelised.

Serve with a few different salads in the summer, such as Gingham Salad (see page 62), Griddled Courgettes with Salsa Verde (see page 64) and/or Buckwheat and Avocado Salad with Fennel and Wild Rose (see page 60), plus a bowl of salad leaves. In autumn and winter, my favourite accompaniment is Sweet Carrots and Savoury Chard (see page 63), root veg mash and a generous helping of buttery peas.

PEA AND BASIL TART WITH A BUTTERY OAT CRUST

Serves 4

Oat flour makes a crisp, buttery crust – the perfect foil for a smooth, basil-scented pea filling and some cool, creamy probiotic labneh. When summer is merely a memory, you can conjure this from a bag of good frozen peas and pretend the evenings are long and light again. Everything in the tart is designed to be easily digested, but you could increase the prebiotic value by adding a garlic clove and using the white part of the spring onions, too.

FOR THE BUTTERY OAT CRUST

70g (2½oz) oat flour (or porridge oats ground in a clean coffee grinder)

70g (2½oz) buckwheat flour

70g (2½oz) ground linseed

2 pinches of sea salt

70g (2½oz) cold salted butter, diced

80–100g (3–4oz) live Greek-style yoghurt

FOR THE PEA AND BASIL FILLING

225g (8oz) frozen peas

3 large organic eggs

150ml (¼ pint) double cream

Finely grated zest of 1 lemon, plus juice of ½ lemon

Large handful of basil, plus extra to dress

3 pinches of sea salt

4 spring onions, green parts only, sliced

120g (4½oz) Labneh (see page 210)

Olive oil, for drizzling

Freshly ground black pepper

Make the oat crust. Put both flours, the ground linseed and salt into a mixing bowl, rub in the butter with your fingertips until it resembles coarse breadcrumbs and then use a butter knife to stir in half of the yoghurt. Add the remaining yoghurt in teaspoons, until the mixture starts to clump together, then gather into a ball and knead until smooth. Form into a disc, wrap and chill in the fridge for 20–30 minutes.

Preheat the oven to 200°C/180°C fan/gas 6 and line the base of a 23cm (9in) loose-based tart tin with a circle of baking parchment.

Lay a sheet of clingfilm on the worktop, place the pastry on top and cover with clingfilm. Roll the pastry into a circle large enough to line the tart tin, peel off the top layer of clingfilm, invert the pastry over the tart tin and ease it into the corners before you remove the clingfilm and trim the top edge with a sharp knife. Keep the scraps in case you need to patch the crust. Chill for at least half an hour.

Line the tart case with baking parchment, fill with baking beans and bake for 15 minutes, then remove the parchment and beans and bake for another 5 minutes. If there are any cracks, soften a bit of the remaining pastry with water and use it as putty to fill them. Set aside. Turn the oven down to 180°C/160°C fan/gas 4.

To make the filling, blanch the peas in a pan of boiling water until they are only just cooked, refresh in cold water, then drain and reserve 25g (1oz). Put the remaining peas into a blender with the eggs, cream, lemon zest and juice, basil and salt. Blend until completely smooth and then pour into the tart case. Scatter the spring onions into the tart with the reserved peas. Bake for 30 minutes, until just set and starting to catch gold at the edges.

Set the tart aside until just warm and then scatter with pieces of labneh and extra basil leaves. Drizzle with olive oil and grind over some black pepper.

BUTTERY SCALLOPS WITH CREAMY AND CRISPY PARSNIPS AND A LUSCIOUS SALAD

Serves 4

A great source of phosphorus, which aids production of digestive enzymes, cell repair and absorption of nutrients, scallops are the ultimate in fast food; mild, succulent and barely in the pan before they are on your plate. This dish should convince even the most ardent fish avoider to give it a try.

FOR THE PARSNIP PURÉE AND CRISPS
800g (1¾lb) parsnips, scrubbed
200ml (7fl oz) double cream
Fresh lemon juice
250g (9oz) lard or dripping
Sea salt and freshly ground black pepper

FOR THE SALAD
300g (11oz) French beans, trimmed
1 ruby Little Gem lettuce
100g (4oz) watercress
½ x quantity Velvet Dressing recipe (see page 226)

FOR THE SCALLOPS
12 fresh scallops, shelled and tough membranes trimmed
1 teaspoon lard, bacon grease or dripping
50g (2oz) unsalted butter
½ lemon, quartered

For the parsnip purée, peel the parsnips, reserve the peelings and set them aside. Chop the parsnips into rough chunks, steam them until very tender, about 10–15 minutes, then drain and mash well (see instructions for the parsnip mash on page 78 for how to achieve a very fine purée). Stir in the cream, a few pinches of salt, lots of black pepper and lemon juice. Thin with a little boiling water if need be. Keep warm.

Make parsnip crisps from the reserved peelings. Heat the lard or dripping in a smallish pan over a medium heat; the lard should come about a third of the way up. When the fat is hot, but not smoking, drop in a piece of peel and check to see that it bubbles and takes at least a minute to brown. Pick up a handful of peelings and drop them carefully into the fat, fry for about 3 minutes until they are light biscuit-coloured and drain on kitchen paper. Repeat to make 4 nests.

For the salad, steam the French beans until just tender, about 4–5 minutes, then plunge into cold water, drain and set aside. Put the beans, lettuce and watercress into a mixing bowl and dress with the velvet dressing, just before you eat.

For the scallops, put them on kitchen paper, sprinkle with a little salt, then top with more kitchen paper and leave for a few minutes. Put a large cast iron frying pan over a high heat and when it is very hot, add the fat and carefully spread it around the pan using a wad of kitchen paper. Add the scallops and let them sear for a minute or so. When the underside forms a brown crust, flip over using a palette knife and sear the other side for 30 seconds. Turn the heat down and add the butter, tip the pan so that the butter flows to the bottom and spoon it over the scallops as it browns – this should take no longer than 30 seconds. Remove while they are still tender and plate up quickly.

Spread some parsnip purée on each plate, add a handful of salad and nestle the scallops into the purée. Top with a nest of parsnip crisps and serve with a piece of lemon.

BLACK RICE NOODLE BOWL

Serves 4

Black rice noodles, bone broth and miso all help to soothe and restore the gut lining and microbiome. The vegetables are entirely your choice; I have chosen easily digestible vegetables that still have a good amount of fibre in them, but if you struggle with asparagus or it is out of season, simply cut a seasonal vegetable that you can tolerate into batons and use this. If you have ribbon pickle, it adds a wonderful sour, gingery zing to this comforting bowl of goodness.

FOR THE BROTH

1 litre (1¾ pints) chicken Bone Broth or Vegetable Broth (see pages 53–54)

4 slices of fresh root ginger

2 garlic cloves, halved (optional)

2 tablespoons red miso paste or genmai miso

FOR THE NOODLE BOWL

4 heaped teaspoons duck, chicken or goose fat

2 large carrots, cut into matchsticks

Tamari, to taste, plus extra to serve

250–280g (9–10oz) black rice noodles (4 noodle cakes)

2 skinless chicken breasts, cut into large chunks

200g (7oz) asparagus spears

2 pak choy, each cut into 6 from top to bottom

4 heaped tablespoons Ribbon Pickle (see page 209) (optional)

8 pink radishes, thinly sliced into coins

4 spring onions, sliced (use green parts only for low FODMAP)

TO SERVE, PER PORTION (OPTIONAL)

½ teaspoon chilli flakes

½ teaspoon Shichimi Togarashi (see page 216)

To make the broth, first heat the broth in a large pan until just simmering, then add the ginger and garlic and simmer for about 20 minutes, while you get on with everything else.

For the noodle bowl, heat 2 heaped teaspoons of the fat in a frying pan and fry the carrot matchsticks over a high heat for a few minutes, until they are just cooked through but still crisp, then tip into a bowl and shake some tamari over them to season. Set aside. Reserve the pan for cooking the chicken.

Bring a small pan of water to the boil, add the black rice noodles, bring back to a simmer, helping the noodles to unfold with a fork, then simmer for 2–3 minutes, until the noodles are just soft. Drain, rinse with cold water and set aside.

Heat the remaining fat in the carrot pan, add the chicken pieces and fry over a medium heat, turning regularly, until they are tinged golden and cooked through, about 5 minutes.

While the chicken fries, cook the vegetables in the broth. Discard the ginger and garlic, bring the broth to a gentle boil, then add the asparagus, followed by the pak choy a minute later. Simmer for 2–3 minutes, until the vegetables are al dente, then lift them out of the broth and set aside. Loosen the miso paste with a little broth and then stir it back into the remaining broth off the heat – do not return to the heat.

To make your noodle bowls, divide the noodles among the bowls, then lay the pak choy and asparagus at one side of each bowl. Place a tangle of carrots, the chicken and a tangle of ribbon pickle on the other side and scatter with radish coins and spring onions. Pour some broth into each bowl and tuck in. Pass around chilli flakes, shichimi togarashi and tamari for those who would like them.

TREATS

TOASTED BUCKWHEAT AND LABNEH CHEESECAKE

RAW SUPERFOOD ICE CREAM

JELLY SWEETS

LINSEED CRACKERS

THUNDER AND LIGHTNING

COCONUT FUDGE POPSICLES

Whether to mark a special birthday or soothe a tough week away, a little treat goes a long way to making life even better. However, sugar can be incredibly inflammatory and so we need our treats to be either savoury or low in sugar, in order that they don't undermine the good work we do with the rest of our diet.

These treats all contain something beneficial: from gelatine to coconut milk or raw egg yolks, they will help to restore the integrity of your gut and make your day a little bit yummier. I find that just knowing there are fudge popsicles in the freezer gives me an enormous sense of wellbeing.

TOASTED BUCKWHEAT AND LABNEH CHEESECAKE

Serves 8

Toasted buckwheat flour and dark muscovado bring depth to the buttery crumb of this simple cheesecake. Labneh is simply yoghurt that has been lightly salted and left to hang for a day or two in muslin, becoming like a tangy cream cheese in the process. While you can't detect the salt, it does give the filling a hint of umami that is pretty much irresistible. Change the berries or fruit according to what is in season.

FOR THE BUCKWHEAT CRUMB
150g (5oz) buckwheat flour
75g (3oz) ground almonds
75g (3oz) dark muscovado sugar
25g (1oz) ground linseed
1 teaspoon ground cinnamon
170g (6oz) cold salted butter, diced

FOR THE LABNEH FILLING
300ml (½ pint) double cream
55g (2oz) light muscovado sugar
½ vanilla pod, split lengthways and seeds scraped out, or 1 teaspoon vanilla extract
250g (9oz) Labneh (see page 210)

350g (12oz) fresh raspberries, to finish

Line a baking sheet with baking parchment. Also line the base of a 23cm (9in) springform cake tin or loose-based tart tin with a circle of baking parchment. Make the buckwheat crumb. Put the flour into a dry frying pan and cook over a medium heat for 5–10 minutes, stirring constantly, until the flour smells toasty. Set aside to cool and then chill in the fridge for about 15 minutes. Meanwhile, preheat the oven to 180°C/160°C fan/gas 4.

Tip the chilled buckwheat flour into a mixing bowl with the ground almonds, dark muscovado sugar, ground linseed and cinnamon. Rub in 100g (4oz) of the butter with your fingertips, until the mixture looks like breadcrumbs. Sprinkle 2–3 tablespoons of water over and gently incorporate with your fingertips – use enough water to give damp clumps, but don't knead the mixture into a dough. Spread it out on the lined baking sheet and bake for 20 minutes, until it feels firm and the edges are tinged with gold (it will crisp up on cooling). Leave to cool completely on the baking sheet.

Gently melt the remaining butter in a pan, then take it off the heat. Break the baked crumble into large crumbs, add to the pan and mix together well. Transfer to the prepared tin and press evenly over the base and up the sides of the tin. Chill in the fridge for at least 30 minutes while you get on with the filling.

To make the filling, pour the cream into a mixing bowl, add the light muscovado sugar and vanilla seeds or extract and stir to combine. Add the labneh and beat with a balloon whisk until stiff but not grainy.

Spread the labneh mixture over the chilled buckwheat base and smooth the top. Finish with a crown of raspberries on top. Chill in the fridge for another hour or so if you can bear it. You can make this 24 hours in advance, but leave the berries until just before you serve it.

RAW SUPERFOOD ICE CREAM

Makes about 850ml (28fl oz) – serves about 6

When I say raw, I mean completely untouched by heat of any kind. Heat changes the nature
of fats and destroys enzymes in the milk and honey that are beneficial for our microbiome.
This luxurious ice cream combines the superfood benefits of raw egg yolks, raw honey and
unpasteurised cream to make a rich and satisfying dessert that your gut will love. Get your eggs
and raw milk from a reputable source to avoid any worry about bacterial contamination.

1 vanilla pod

3 large organic egg yolks*

75–100g (3–4oz) raw honey

2 teaspoons brandy or vodka (or
use vanilla extract, but leave out the
vanilla pod)

750ml (24fl oz) double cream
(ideally unpasteurised)*

*Raw eggs or unpasteurised dairy
should not be eaten by those who
are pregnant, immunodeficient or
by children under three.

Split the vanilla pod with a sharp knife and scrape the seeds into a bowl.
(Put the pod into a jar of sugar or honey to flavour it, or whizz it up in a
clean coffee grinder with some muscovado sugar to make vanilla powder.)

Whisk the vanilla seeds, egg yolks, honey and alcohol together until they
are thick and mousse-like. Stir in the cream, taste for sweetness (add more
honey if needed) and then churn in an ice-cream maker.

If you don't have an ice-cream maker, you can make your own Victorian-
style ice cream churn by putting a 1.5-litre (2½ pint) Kilner jar into a
large bowl filled with ice cubes. Pour a bag of table salt over the ice cubes
and pour your ice cream mixture into the jar. Stir leisurely with a spatula,
scraping the sides as you go, until the ice cream is thick and then transfer
to a container and freezer until firm. The exothermic reaction of salt on ice
makes the ice super cold – enough to chill your ice cream while you stir it.
This produces ice cream almost as smooth as the kind made in an ice-cream
maker – with a bit of science thrown in! You can only churn a half batch
mixture in this way, so have two ice-filled bowls ready, or just make half
the mixture.

Once the ice cream is ready, serve it immediately (or freeze for up to
a month and soften in the fridge for 30 minutes prior to serving – the
freshly made ice cream will have the smoothest texture). Serve scoops of
ice cream in small bowls with some fresh berries, or drizzle with Magic
Chocolate Coating (see Coconut Fudge Popsicles on page 104) and
sprinkle with toasted flaked almonds.

JELLY SWEETS

Makes about 36 of each type

When I was small, my mum would always give me a square of raw jelly to chew while she made up the remainder. It turns out that the gelatine part of those little treats was good for repairing my gut – although the sugar wasn't!

You can use any seasonal fruit that your digestion will tolerate, just sieve out pips and sweeten with raw honey before measuring the amount. For a truly soothing treat, choose the milky coconut version, reminiscent of Turkish delight; the raw honey provides food for your microbes and a little training for your immune system, while cardamom and rose both bring calm.

FOR THE FRUIT JELLIES
300ml (½ pint) fruit purée sweetened with raw honey (see method)

2 teaspoons rose water or 1 teaspoon vanilla extract (optional)

50g (2oz) leaf gelatine

FOR THE COCONUT AND CARDAMOM JELLIES
300ml (½ pint) coconut milk

5 tablespoons raw honey

2 tablespoons rose water

5 green cardamom pods, seeds removed and ground finely

Good pinch of sea salt

50g (2oz) leaf gelatine

For the fruit jellies, make your purée first out of any soft fruit by blending it and then passing through a sieve to remove any seeds. Sweeten to taste with raw honey, if it needs it, then flavour with rose water (to taste) or vanilla extract (if using).

For the coconut jellies, whisk together the coconut milk, honey, rose water (to taste), ground cardamom and salt. Sieve out the cardamom if you don't want to see it in the jelly.

For both types of jellies, soak the gelatine leaves in cold water for about 5 minutes and then gently squeeze the water out and pop into a pan on its own. Melt the gelatine over a very low heat and as soon as it is completely liquid, stir in the fruit purée or coconut mixture and whisk until completely smooth.

Pour into silicone ice cube trays or a large square-sided container, lined with waxed paper or clingfilm, and chill in the fridge for a couple of hours, until set.

Once set, dip the bottom of the ice cube trays or container into hot water for 20–30 seconds to melt the outside of the jellies a little and then pop out onto a chopping board. Slice up the slab into pieces and store the jellies on baking parchment in an airtight box in the fridge for up to a week.

LINSEED CRACKERS

Makes about 25

Baking brings out the nutty flavour of linseed, which is both prebiotic and soothing for the gut. A clean coffee grinder is essential to get your linseed really fine, and roll the crackers as thin as you can to get them really crisp. You can substitute most flours for the teff flour in this recipe and it will still work; for gluten free, try sorghum, chestnut, millet or buckwheat, but if gluten isn't an issue, rye or spelt also work well. Go to town with your flavourings – they are all beneficial!

FOR THE CRACKERS

60g (2¼oz) whole golden linseeds

120g (4½oz) boiling water

40g (1½oz) ground golden linseed

60g (2¼oz) brown teff flour or other flour, plus extra for dusting

40g (1½oz) chia seeds (or sesame seeds)

1 teaspoon olive oil

3 tablespoons finely grated Parmesan (or ½ teaspoon sea salt)

Flaky sea salt, to sprinkle (optional)

TO FLAVOUR THE CRACKERS

Spices – ground cumin, turmeric or cinnamon; chilli powder or smoked paprika; coriander, fennel, celery, dill, anise or cardamom seeds

Herbs – fresh rosemary or sage; dried oregano or rose petals

Fresh – finely grated lemon or orange zest; finely chopped garlic

Seeds – sesame, poppy or chia seeds; ground pumpkin or sunflower seeds

Preheat the oven to 180°C/160°C fan/gas 4. You'll also need two or three unlined baking sheets. For the crackers, put the whole linseeds into a small heatproof bowl and pour over the boiling water. Leave for 10 minutes to soak up the water and form a gel.

Put the ground linseed, teff flour, chia seeds, olive oil and Parmesan into a mixing bowl and scrape in the soaked linseeds. Use your hands to squidge into a firm dough. If the dough feels too sticky, put a little flour on the work surface and knead for a minute, or if it's too crumbly, add a little water.

Grind or finely chop whatever flavourings you are adding to the dough. Knead your chosen ingredients into the dough, either into the whole piece, or divide the dough into three pieces and flavour each one separately. Add about 2–3 teaspoons of your flavouring to the whole piece of dough.

To roll out the crackers, tear off a piece of baking parchment the size of your baking sheets, or use flexible silicone baking mats. Sprinkle a little flour over the parchment or mat, place a third of the dough on top and cover with a sheet of clingfilm. Roll out to the depth of the seeds, as thin as it will go. Repeat with the remaining dough.

If you like, sprinkle the crackers with extra seeds and a little flaky sea salt, then replace the clingfilm and gently roll these into the dough. You can mark the dough into long thin crackers with a pizza cutter, or break it up after baking if you don't have one, as a knife can tear the delicate dough.

Transfer to the baking sheets (on parchment or mats) and bake for about 15 minutes, until golden and crisp – if there is any flex in the centre when you press, put them back in the oven again. Cool completely on the parchment or mats and then carefully peel off and break the crackers into rustic shards. Store in an airtight box for up to 10 days.

THUNDER AND LIGHTNING

Serves 4

So often, when you have to give things up, it feels like blow-out desserts are off the menu. This one isn't too high in sugar, but it is crazy delicious – a little like tiramisu with that wonderful combination of bitter coffee and softly whipped cream. If you have a gluten-free birthday coming up, try doubling the cake, brush with the coffee syrup and fill it with coffee rippled whipped cream.

125g (4½oz) hazelnuts

110g (4¼oz) organic eggs (about 2 large eggs)

75g (3oz) light muscovado sugar

Pinch of sea salt

25g (1oz) chestnut flour (or white teff or buckwheat flour)

100ml (3½fl oz) cold espresso coffee (decaffeinated, if you prefer)

2 tablespoons date or maple syrup

375ml (13fl oz) double cream

1 teaspoon vanilla extract

Line the base of a 20cm (8in) deep-sided cake tin with baking parchment. Don't grease or line the sides. Preheat the oven to 200°C/180°C fan/gas 6. You will also need a serving dish, about 24cm (9½in) square or similar.

First, toast your hazelnuts in a dry frying pan over a low heat, shaking the nuts frequently so that they cook evenly. When the skins have cracked and they are kissed all over with gold, about 20 minutes, tip them into a clean tea towel and rub the skins off. Reserve 50g (2oz) for the top and grind the remainder as finely as you can using a clean coffee grinder or blender.

In a mixing bowl or stand mixer, whisk the eggs, 65g (2¼oz) of the sugar and the salt together for 6–7 minutes, until tripled in volume, light-coloured and a thick rope of mixture falls and dissolves slowly on the surface. If doing this by hand, it will take quite a bit longer.

Tip the ground hazelnuts and chestnut flour into a sieve and sift half over the whisked eggs, fold in gently but thoroughly, then sift in the remainder, folding deftly just until you can't see any dry flour. Scrape the batter into the prepared cake tin and spread out gently. Bake for about 20–25 minutes, until the cake has risen and settled and feels just firm to touch but hasn't shrunk away from the sides. A cake tester inserted in the centre should come out clean.

Cool completely in the tin, then turn out onto a wire rack. Break the cake into bite-sized chunks and cover the base of your serving dish with it. Mix the coffee and syrup together, taste for sweetness (it should be bitter, but pleasantly so) and drizzle over the cake – it should be moist, but not sodden, so use only as much as you need.

Stir the remaining sugar into the cream with the vanilla extract and whip to soft peaks, then spoon this over the cake chunks. Roughly chop the reserved hazelnuts and scatter over the top. You can eat this immediately, but it is better after an hour or so in the fridge. Let it come back to room temperature for 15 minutes before serving.

COCONUT FUDGE POPSICLES

Makes 6–7

When I first made these, I was amazed that something with so few ingredients could be so unbelievably good! Medjool dates have a fudgy quality that gives the popsicles an ice cream texture and rich butterscotch flavour. Although the clean eating brigade have taken coconut as their mascot, it does have verifiable healing qualities, being rich in lauric acid that supports gut healing and immune function. Coconut kefir works too for a probiotic hit, but if you're not a fan of coconut, try them with half yoghurt or milk kefir and half double cream.

6–8 medjool dates, stoned

400ml (14fl oz) coconut milk

2 teaspoons vanilla extract or seeds from 1 vanilla pod

Pinch of sea salt

FOR THE MAGIC CHOCOLATE COATING (OPTIONAL)

25g (1oz) toasted flaked almonds, shelled pistachio nuts, desiccated coconut or freeze-dried raspberries, to coat

125g (4½oz) dark chocolate, roughly chopped

3 tablespoons coconut oil (or unsalted butter)

Put the dates into a blender with the coconut milk, vanilla extract or seeds and salt and blend until completely smooth. If the mixture is less than velvety smooth, pass it through a sieve to remove any really fibrous bits.

Pour into popsicle moulds, pop the tops on and freeze for at least 3 hours, preferably overnight. If you are using popsicle moulds with sticks, freeze the popsicles for about an hour until slushy, then push the sticks in and continue freezing. To unmould the popsicles, run the outside under hot water for a few seconds and pull the stick to release.

If you like, you can dip the popsicles into melted chocolate for an all-out chocolate fudge popsicle party. Finely chop any nuts if you are using and put any other sprinkles onto little plates. Melt the chocolate and coconut oil in a heatproof bowl over a pan of barely simmering water, stir to combine, then set aside to cool to tepid while you unmould your popsicles.

Dip each popsicle briefly into the melted chocolate and straight away into your sprinkles before it sets. Hold for a few seconds more and then pop it on a tray in the freezer, while you repeat with the rest. You will have some chocolate coating left over, so just keep it in a jar and re-use for when you make some Raw Superfood Ice Cream (see page 99).

The coated and uncoated popsicles will keep in the freezer for up to a month (if they last that long!)

NOURISH

BREAKFASTS

FOUR-GRAIN PORRIDGE

TOASTY BUCKWHEAT GRANOLA

BAKED BEANS ON TOAST

GLOBE ARTICHOKE AND SALSIFY TORTILLA

FARINATA

SHAKSHUKA WITH BROAD BEANS AND LABNEH

SOURDOUGH TOAST WITH BROAD BEAN HUMMUS, FETA AND MINT

TEFF AND SESAME PANCAKES

SOURDOUGH TOAST WITH SUNFLOWER SEED BUTTER AND PLUM COMPOTE

After a good 12 hours without food, your microbes are seriously hungry, so here are some breakfasts full of prebiotic nourishment to keep both you and your gut flora full all morning.

I love to fill the freezer with home-made baked beans and teff pancakes, the cupboard with granola, artichoke hearts and sunflower seed butter, and keep a pot of porridge or tub of hummus in the fridge for instant breakfasts through the week.

At the weekend, I might throw together a breakfast tortilla, or make crispy farinata for a leisurely brunch after a morning run, when I have time to spread the papers out and take my time.

FOUR-GRAIN PORRIDGE

Serves 4

Because none of these grains are rolled or cracked, the porridge has a succulent risotto texture that is particularly satisfying. Oat groats and brown rice are plump, while teff and amaranth are tiny, but all are packed with nutrients, fibre, protein and resistant starch that give the porridge a slightly earthy, richer flavour. I use maple or date syrup to sweeten, because honey tends to make the porridge thin and runny. If you can buy raw (unpasteurised) milk, the enzymes that this contains will make your porridge all the more nourishing.

100g (4oz) oat groats

100g (4oz) short grain brown rice

70g (2½oz) teff grain

40g (1½oz) amaranth grain

1 tablespoon live natural yoghurt

350–400ml (12–14fl oz) raw milk* or home-made Nut Milk (see page 237), plus extra to serve

3–4 teaspoons maple or date syrup (optional)

1 tablespoon salted butter

½ teaspoon ground cinnamon

TO SERVE

4 large handfuls of fresh berries or roast fruit

Carob molasses (optional)

*Unpasteurised dairy should not be eaten by those who are pregnant, immunodeficient or by children under three.

Put the oat groats, rice and teff and amaranth grains into a large jar or bowl, then stir in the yoghurt and 700ml (1¼ pints) water. Cover and leave at room temperature for 12–24 hours.

In the morning, transfer the mixture to a pan and cook gently until the oats and rice are soft and the water has been almost completely absorbed, stirring often to prevent sticking. Add most of the milk, the syrup, butter and cinnamon and cook gently until the porridge has a risotto consistency (add more milk, if you like). Don't let it boil or the milk will taste burnt.

Serve topped with fresh or roast fruit, a splash of milk and a drizzle of carob molasses (if using). Because this porridge contains rice, any leftovers must be cooled quickly and eaten within 48 hours. If you would like to keep it longer, just freeze in portions for up to a month and reheat from frozen.

TOASTY BUCKWHEAT GRANOLA

*Makes about 1.4kg (3lb 1oz) — servings depend on how much you eat and how you use it
(i.e. as a complete breakfast or as a sprinkle)*

Buckwheat groats are rinsed to remove the soapy coating that can interfere with digestion and then toasted in a low oven to become possibly the crunchiest, nuttiest granola ever. Just sweet enough to feel treaty and full of delicious roast and raw nuts, you can sprinkle this over yoghurt, fruit or just straight into your mouth when you crave a little crunch. Customise the nuts and dried fruit to your taste and try a little nutmeg in place of cinnamon.

400g (14oz) buckwheat groats

4 tablespoons olive oil (or melted coconut oil or butter)

100ml (3½fl oz) maple or date syrup

4 teaspoons vanilla extract

1 teaspoon ground cinnamon (optional)

3 pinches of sea salt

400g (14oz) flaked almonds

120g (4½oz) buckwheat, teff, oat or rye flour

60g (2¼oz) ground linseed

150g (5oz) shelled pistachio nuts, left whole

150g (5oz) walnuts, roughly broken up

50g (2oz) dried barberries, sour cherries or tart currants

Preheat the oven to 140°C/120°C fan/gas 1. Line three baking trays with baking parchment and line a roasting tray with a double thickness of kitchen paper. Soak the buckwheat groats in cold water for 5 minutes, then rinse them in a sieve until the water runs clear. Drain well and then tip onto the kitchen paper, cover with another layer of paper, rub the groats to dry them a little and then tip onto two of the parchment-lined baking trays, spreading evenly. Bake for about 40–60 minutes, until dry and crunchy.

Whisk together the olive oil, syrup, vanilla extract, cinnamon and salt in a mixing bowl, add the toasted buckwheat groats and flaked almonds, mix well, then add the flour and ground linseed and mix again. Divide evenly between the three parchment-lined baking trays (re-using the original paper) and spread each portion out into a layer of clumps.

Bake for about an hour, turning the trays around halfway through. The granola should be almost completely dry by this stage, but not too golden. Break up any big clusters that seem soft in the middle and bake for another 15–30 minutes, until crisp and deeply golden. The granola will continue to crisp up as it cools, so if in doubt, take some out and leave to cool before deciding whether it is cooked.

Cool completely on the baking trays, then tip the granola into a clean mixing bowl, add the pistachios, walnuts and dried berries or fruit and mix well. Store in an airtight container and use within a couple of weeks.

BAKED BEANS ON TOAST

Makes about 800g (1¾lb) – serves about 6

The British have a unique fondness for the humble baked bean that the remainder of Europe puzzle over. Although beans in general are perfect microbial food, commercial baked beans contain a lot of sugar, which makes them less than ideal for a happy gut. My version gives a nod to the meatiness of Boston baked beans as I cook them in bone broth, but remains true to the simplicity of a smooth tomato sauce with that comforting sweetness coming from a few dates.

300g (11oz) dried haricot beans

750–850ml (24–28fl oz) chicken or pork Bone Broth (see page 53)

1 bay leaf

2 teaspoons bacon, chicken or duck fat or lard

1 large carrot, finely chopped

½ celery stick, finely chopped

1 onion, finely chopped

2 garlic cloves, finely chopped

Few pinches of sea salt

7–8 dried dates, stoned and finely chopped

300g (11oz) tinned chopped tomatoes with their juice

Few dashes of Worcestershire sauce, to taste

1 tablespoon cider vinegar

Toasted sourdough bread and salted butter, to serve

Soak the haricot beans overnight in plenty of cold water. Drain the soaked beans, then put into a pan and cover with fresh cold water. Bring to the boil and boil rapidly for 10 minutes, skimming off any froth that rises. Drain and rinse, then return to the pan with 550ml (19fl oz) of the bone broth and the bay leaf. Cover with a lid, bring to the boil, then simmer until the beans are just tender but not collapsing, about 45–60 minutes. Drain and reserve the liquid and beans separately, discarding the bay leaf.

Meanwhile, to make the sauce, heat the fat in a pan, then add the chopped vegetables, garlic and salt. Sauté gently for about 20 minutes, stirring occasionally, until the vegetables are soft, sweet and just starting to colour.

Add the dates and tomatoes to the pan, turn up the heat and stir constantly as the juices evaporate. When the mixture smells sweet, add the reserved bean liquid, a further 200ml (7fl oz) of the bone broth, the Worcestershire sauce and cider vinegar. Cover and bring back to the boil, then cook for another 15 minutes or so.

Mash the tomato mixture with a potato masher in the pan, or purée in a blender for a completely smooth sauce. Taste for salt, Worcestershire sauce or vinegar, adding a little more, if you like. Return the sauce to the pan (if you puréed it), add the beans, then cover and cook undisturbed over a lowish heat for another 15–20 minutes. Check the liquid levels at this point and either add some more broth, or leave the lid off and continue cooking to thicken up the sauce. Serve the beans in their sauce with some lavishly buttered sourdough toast and a large cup of tea.

Cool any leftover baked beans and store in a lidded container in the fridge for 3–4 days. You may need to add a little liquid when you heat them again, but remember that cold broth will set and make them seem drier until warmed through. Freeze any you won't eat within that time for up to 3 months.

GLOBE ARTICHOKE AND SALSIFY TORTILLA

Serves 4

A tortilla is essentially a crustless quiche made in a frying pan, a wonderful vehicle for any leftover veg and a perfect portable breakfast. If you are brave enough to turn it out halfway through cooking and slide it back into the pan, you will get a golden crust all the way around, but you can just finish it under the grill. Artichoke and salsify make my version of the Spanish classic much more fun for your microbes and if you eat it cold, then it also contains some bonus resistant starch. I love both dill and tarragon here, so choose your own favourite.

3–4 fat salsify or scorzonera roots (about 200g peeled weight)

Squeeze of fresh lemon juice

1 tablespoon olive oil

4 fat spring onions, sliced

180g (6oz) artichoke hearts in oil, drained and sliced

6 large organic eggs

250g (9oz) cooked and cooled salad potatoes, roughly diced

15g (½oz) dill fronds or 7g (¼oz) tarragon leaves, finely chopped

1 teaspoon lard or duck fat

Sea salt and freshly ground black pepper

Scrub, peel and slice the salsify roots and drop them into a bowl of water with the squeeze of lemon juice added, then drain and steam for about 10 minutes, until tender. If you undercook salsify it will turn grey as it cools. Set aside.

Heat the olive oil in a cast iron or non-stick frying pan, add the spring onions and soften gently for about 5–6 minutes, until they smell sweet. Add the artichoke hearts and steamed salsify and warm through for a few minutes.

Beat the eggs in a mixing bowl with 3–4 pinches of salt and lots of black pepper, then stir in the potatoes, herbs and everything from the frying pan. Wipe out the pan with some kitchen paper and put it back over a high heat with ½ teaspoon of the lard or duck fat. Swirl the fat around the pan and then pour in the tortilla mixture, pressing down the vegetables to make a roughly even surface. Turn the heat down to low and cook for about 8–10 minutes, until the edges look set, but the top is still a little runny.

Place a plate (slightly larger in diameter) on top of the pan, then using oven gloves, grasp the pan and plate together and flip the whole thing over so that the tortilla is on the plate. Return the pan to the heat, turn up to high again and melt the remaining lard or duck fat. Slide the tortilla back into the pan and tuck any loose edges under. Turn the heat down to low and cook for another 5 minutes, then tip the tortilla out onto a plate as before. Leave to cool and set for at least 15 minutes before serving, and eat at room temperature.

FARINATA

Serves 4

Farinata is a fermented chickpea flatbread with a crisp exterior and soft interior, a bit like a thick, savoury pancake – it is perfect for scooping things up and dipping into olive oil. Fermenting makes the chickpea flour easier to digest, and the longer you let it ferment, the more tangy the flavour will be; don't let it ferment for more than 12 hours at room temperature though, or the mixture may go bad.

75g (3oz) chickpea flour (or fava bean or yellow pea flour)

75g (3oz) millet, teff or chickpea flour

60g (2¼oz) Sourdough Starter (see pages 35–37) or live natural yoghurt

230g (8oz) tepid water

3 tablespoons olive oil

½ teaspoon sea salt

1 heaped teaspoon duck fat, lard or coconut oil

Scattering of herb leaves (picked from their stems), such as rosemary or thyme

TO SERVE

100g (4oz) rocket leaves, rinsed and patted dry

150g (5oz) cherry tomatoes, halved

150g (5oz) smoked salmon or gravadlax, torn into pieces

Nigella seeds, for sprinkling

Tahini Sauce (see page 224)

Olive oil

Lemon wedges

In a mixing bowl, beat together the flours, sourdough starter or yoghurt and tepid water with a whisk, until smooth. Cover and set aside at room temperature for 6–12 hours. If you need to leave it longer, after 6 hours put it into the fridge for up to 48 hours.

When the time is up, put a large, heavy-based, ovenproof frying pan or heavy roasting tray into the oven and preheat the oven to 240°C/220°C fan/gas 9.

Whisk the olive oil and salt into the chickpea mixture until incorporated. When the oven is up to temperature, take the pan or roasting tray out and put the fat into it. Once the fat has melted, pour in the chickpea mixture, scatter with the herbs and a little more salt if you like, then bake for 12–15 minutes, until it's tinged golden, crisp at the edges and firm to the touch.

To serve, tear up the farinata and scatter over a serving plate, top with the rocket and cherry tomatoes then scatter over the pieces of salmon and sprinkle with nigella seeds. Serve with the tahini sauce, olive oil and lemon wedges.

SHAKSHUKA WITH BROAD BEANS AND LABNEH

Serves 8

In every part of the world you can find a breakfast based on eggs and tomatoes, all rich with umami and wonderfully sustaining. What makes shakshuka stand out for me is the sweetness of slowly cooked onions and that subtle background note of cumin and chilli. I add broad beans and artichokes to mine for a green prebiotic kick, but you can also try French beans, steamed kale, chard or fresh peas. If you don't have labneh, then really thick live Greek-style yoghurt will do and you can still hang it up overnight to firm up. Although it might seem like a lot of work for breakfast, if you make the tomatoes in advance it can take as little as 10 minutes to get this on the table and it will totally set you up for the day.

4 tablespoons olive oil

1 teaspoon cumin seeds

Pinch of dried chilli flakes

2 bay leaves

2 large red onions, roughly chopped

Pinch of sea salt

800g (1¾lb) tinned chopped tomatoes with their juice

500g (1lb 2oz) broad beans (weight in their pods), podded

4 large organic eggs

150g (5oz) artichoke hearts in oil, drained and sliced

Large handful of flat-leaf parsley, roughly chopped

180g (6oz) Labneh (see page 210)

Wholemeal flatbread or Teff and Sesame Pancakes (see page 122), to serve (optional)

First make the tomato sauce – this can be done up to 48 hours in advance (once made, simply cool and chill in the fridge, then reheat before serving). Put the olive oil, cumin seeds, chilli flakes and bay leaves into a large lidded frying pan and cook gently for a few minutes. Add the red onions and salt, then cook very gently for at least 15 minutes, until the onions are soft, sweet smelling and pale pink. Add the tomatoes, put the lid on the pan and leave the sauce to simmer gently for about an hour, stirring occasionally, and adding a little water if it gets too thick. Discard the bay leaves.

When the sauce is almost done, steam the broad beans for 3–4 minutes, until just tender, then refresh in cold water and set aside. If you are feeling generous, you can slip the beans out of their grey skins, but they do provide some nice roughage if you keep them on.

Make an indentation in the tomato sauce and crack an egg into it, repeating for all four eggs. Simmer gently, uncovered, for a few minutes while the white starts to turn opaque, then cover and simmer for a few more minutes, until the white is cooked through but the yolk is still runny.

Serve each person with an egg and its sauce, scattered with broad beans, artichoke hearts and parsley. Dot each plate with pieces of labneh and tuck in. Serve with flatbread or pancakes, if you like.

SOURDOUGH TOAST WITH BROAD BEAN HUMMUS, FETA AND MINT

Serves 4

Broad beans make a really creamy, fresh hummus that absolutely sings with tart feta and cool mint. Many people find broad beans easier to digest than dried pulses, so I like to think of this as a gateway hummus. You can adjust the level of garlic to suit your tummy; add an extra clove and also rub some on your toast for maximum punch, or use Garlic Oil (see page 225) in place of the olive oil and leave out the whole garlic for something that is much more soothing, if a little less prebiotic.

1kg (2¼lb) broad beans in their pods or 300g frozen broad beans

1 tablespoon tahini

1–2 garlic cloves, finely chopped

100ml (3½fl oz) olive oil, plus extra for drizzling

Juice of 1 lemon

1 teaspoon fine sea salt

20g (¾oz) dill fronds, finely chopped (optional)

TO SERVE

4 large or 8 small slices of sourdough bread

1 plump garlic clove, halved

120g (4½oz) feta cheese

Handful of mint leaves, chopped

Pod the broad beans (or use straight from frozen), then steam for 3–4 minutes, until tender. Refresh with cold water and tip into a blender. Add the tahini, garlic, olive oil, half of the lemon juice and the salt and blend in bursts, scraping down, until the mixture is quite well broken down.

Add about 50ml (2fl oz) of water and blend again until the mixture looks smooth and creamy. Taste and decide whether you want to add the remaining lemon juice and possibly some more water, until the hummus is the texture of whipped cream.

Stir the dill (if using) into the hummus, check for salt and then scrape into a container or use right away. Any leftovers will keep in the fridge for a few days in a clean jar with oil poured on top to exclude the air.

To serve, toast the bread slices (on a griddle pan is nice, if you have one). Rub each slice with the garlic (or leave it out if you're sensitive) and drizzle over a little olive oil. Spread hummus generously on the toast, crumble the feta over the hummus, scatter with mint, then finish with another drizzle of olive oil. Eat in the sunshine if possible.

TEFF AND SESAME PANCAKES

Serves 4 (Makes about 8–10 pancakes)

A tiny, nutritional powerhouse of a grain, teff is packed with resistant starch, prebiotic fibre, iron, magnesium and calcium. Teff has a malty, savoury flavour akin to rye flour, which you can use as an alternative in this recipe. I soak the pancakes overnight with some yoghurt or sourdough starter to make silky pancakes that are easier to digest.

300ml (½ pint) milk or dairy-free milk

130g (4½oz) brown teff, rye or oat flour

1 tablespoon live natural yoghurt or Sourdough Starter (see pages 35–37)

2 large organic eggs

Large pinch of sea salt

50g (2oz) black or white sesame seeds

Clarified butter, duck fat, lard or coconut oil, for frying

At least 6 hours before you plan to make your pancakes, whisk together the milk, flour and yoghurt or sourdough starter. Cover and leave at room temperature for at least 6 hours or up to 24 hours.

When you are ready to make the pancakes, whisk in the eggs, salt and sesame seeds. Check that the batter is not too thick and add a little more milk if it is – you'll know after your first pancake either way!

Heat a heavy-based frying pan over a medium heat. Brush lightly with fat, or use a wad of kitchen paper to give you a nice thin coating. Pour in some pancake batter and swirl it around the pan to give you a thin crêpe. When the underneath is golden brown, about 2–3 minutes, loosen gently with a palette knife and flip over to cook the other side briefly, about 1 minute. Keep warm in a low oven (if you are eating them immediately), while you cook the remainder in the same way, and pop a piece of greaseproof paper between each pancake to stop them sticking together.

These pancakes freeze beautifully for a month or two and are great to have stashed in the freezer for impromptu wraps, burritos and chimichangas. Just let them defrost at room temperature for 10 minutes or pop into a dry frying pan and reheat from frozen.

Although these pancakes are delicious for breakfast with some fruit and yoghurt, they also make a great alternative to flatbreads for scooping up hummus (see Broad Bean Hummus on page 120) or curry, to accompany Shakshuka (see page 119), or for making Teff Burritos (see page 163).

SOURDOUGH TOAST WITH SUNFLOWER SEED BUTTER AND PLUM COMPOTE

Makes about 325g (11½oz) sunflower seed butter and 750g (1lb 10oz) plum compote

This is a very gut-friendly take on that American classic, peanut butter and jam. Sunflower seeds make the most delicious spread for your morning toast, richly satisfying and full of fibre and soothing essential fats. If you have a high-speed blender then you can get a silky smooth mixture, but it will still taste good if not. The compote works just as well with greengages, peaches, apricots, figs and berries.

250g (9oz) sunflower seeds

50g (2oz) coconut oil (or other cold-pressed oil)

2–4 tablespoons cold-pressed sunflower or rapeseed oil

½ teaspoon fine sea salt

750g (1lb 10oz) plums, quartered and stoned

2–3 tablespoons date or maple syrup, raw honey or muscovado sugar

2 teaspoons vanilla extract

Sourdough toast, to serve

Gently toast the sunflower seeds in a dry frying pan over a low heat for 7–10 minutes, stirring frequently, until they are touched with gold and smell deliciously nutty. Tip onto a plate and cool for 5 minutes or so, then put them into a blender with the coconut oil, 2 tablespoons of the sunflower or rapeseed oil and the salt. Blend, stopping to scrape down as necessary, until the mixture is completely smooth. If you would like the consistency to be more like tahini, add the remaining oil and blend to mix.

Scrape the sunflower seed butter into a clean jar and leave to cool, then close up the jar and store in the cupboard for up to a month.

Put the plums into a large pan with the syrup or sugar and vanilla extract. If you are using honey, leave this out and add it later when the plums are cool, to retain its benefits. Cook the plums over a medium heat, stirring occasionally as the juices start to run and they break down a little. When all the plums feel soft, about 15 minutes, check for sweetness and then scrape the compote into a large jar or bowl. Cool, then stir in the honey now (if using). Cover and keep in the fridge for 5–6 days.

To serve, spread the toast with sunflower seed butter and top with compote. Sunflower seed butter can also be used in place of tahini or peanut butter in many recipes.

SOUPS

ROAST ONION SOUP WITH BARLEY

CREAMY NETTLE AND WILD GARLIC SOUP

TURKISH LEEK SOUP WITH SMOKY BUTTER

COCONUT AND CAULIFLOWER SOUP WITH MUSSELS

CAVOLO NERO AND CANNELLINI BEAN SOUP

JERUSALEM ARTICHOKE SOUP WITH TOASTED ALMONDS

BLACK BEAN SOUP

If you think that a bowl of soup is not a meal, then think again, because these soups are deeply flavoursome, rich and filling. The bone broth, alliums, brassicas and beans that sustain our microbes are also incredibly satisfying for us, with lots of the fibre that keeps us fuller for longer.

You may want to accompany them with a hunk of crusty bread and butter to mop up the last drops (if you can resist licking the bowl clean).

ROAST ONION SOUP WITH BARLEY

Serves 4

Roast onions are both savoury and sweet but also bitter where the edges catch and full of umami. This soup is a doddle to make, richly creamy with a wonderful contrast from crisp red onions and chewy barley. Full of prebiotic fibre and rich in minerals and gelatine, this is an incredibly satisfying way to feed your microbes.

50g (2oz) barley groats (or short grain brown rice)

1.4kg (3lb 1oz) white onions (about 8), each cut into 8 wedges

2 red onions, each cut into 12 wedges

4 tablespoons duck or goose fat

Few pinches of sea salt

60g (2¼oz) salted butter

500g (1lb 2oz) floury potatoes (peeled if you like), cut into small dice

4 celery sticks, cut into small dice

2 carrots, cut into small dice

1 large or 2 small bay leaves

1.5 litres (2½ pints) chicken Bone Broth (see page 53)

Few chives, finely snipped

Mild dried chilli flakes (Turkish dried chilli flakes are good) or black pepper

24 hours before you make the soup, cover the barley (or rice) with water and set aside at room temperature. When you are ready to make the soup, drain the barley, put it into a pan and cover with lots of water. Simmer until it is soft, about 30–45 minutes, then drain and reserve.

Preheat the oven to 200°C/180°C fan/gas 6. Spread the white onions over two baking sheets, and the red onions over a third, then dot with the duck or goose fat and sprinkle with the salt. Roast for 30 minutes and then remove any crisp pieces to a plate, turn the onions over and roast for another 10–15 minutes, until the red onion wedges are crisply caramelised and the white onions tinged golden brown. Loosen the onions from the baking sheets with a palette knife before they get seriously stuck, then set aside for a moment.

While the onions roast, melt the butter in a pan, add the potatoes, celery, carrots and bay leaf and sauté for 15–20 minutes, scraping the potatoes off the bottom of the pan as they catch and caramelise, until everything is soft and sweet smelling. Pour in the bone broth and simmer for 15 minutes, then set aside to cool for 10 minutes.

Put the roast white onions into a blender with the liquid from the vegetables and half of the vegetables, reserving the remainder. Blend until the soup is velvety smooth, taste for seasoning and add extra salt if you think it needs it. Stir the soup and reserved vegetables together and return to the pan to heat through gently.

Serve the soup with the barley on top, along with a little crown of crisp red onions. Sprinkle the chives over with a good pinch of chilli flakes or a grind of black pepper per bowl.

Some buttered sourdough is a great accompaniment.

CREAMY NETTLE AND WILD GARLIC SOUP

Serves 4

The scent of wild garlic is an unmistakable sign that spring is truly here and it's time to don my rubber gloves to gather some tender nettle tops for a nourishing soup. Rich with iron, this deeply green tonic feels amazingly restorative after root- and cabbage-heavy winter meals. Foraging is a great way to take in some new microbes, but choose leaves that don't enjoy too much attention from dogs, or give them a good rinse before you eat them.

50g (2oz) salted butter

Bunch of spring onions, roughly sliced

1 leek, white part only, washed and roughly sliced

300g (11oz) potatoes, peeled (if you like) and diced

750ml (24fl oz) Bone Broth (see page 53)

500g (1lb 2oz) nettle tops (half a carrier bagful), washed and tough stalks discarded

2 large handfuls of wild garlic leaves

200ml (7fl oz) double cream

Good squeeze of fresh lemon juice

Few pinches of sea salt

Good grind of black pepper

Pinch or two of ground nutmeg

Garlicky Almond Migas (see page 215), to finish

Melt the butter in a large pan over a medium heat, then add the spring onions and leek and cook gently for about 10–15 minutes, until they smell caramel sweet and are starting to colour.

Add the potatoes to the pan with the bone broth. Bring to the boil, then cover and simmer until the potatoes are soft, about 20 minutes. Add the nettles to the pan and bring back to the boil, then simmer for another 5 minutes or so, until the nettles are tender. Let the soup cool a little before you blend it.

Pour the soup into a blender with half of the wild garlic leaves, 150ml (¼ pint) of the cream, the lemon juice, salt, black pepper and nutmeg. Whizz until velvety smooth and then check to see if it needs more lemon juice, salt, pepper or nutmeg. Thin with a little boiling water if it is too thick.

To serve, reheat the soup gently but don't let it boil. Finely chop the remaining wild garlic leaves and use these to garnish the soup with a swirl of the remaining cream. Pass the bowl of migas for people to add to their soup.

TURKISH LEEK SOUP WITH SMOKY BUTTER

Serves 4

This creamy soup is a doddle to make and yet the flavours are rich and complex. It really pays to cook the leek slowly and let it become sweet and mellow – this can be done up to 24 hours in advance. Smoky butter is so delicious it would make a piece of cardboard taste good, but swirled into this soup, it's sublime. If you don't have Turkish chilli flakes, use a teaspoon of paprika instead. Leeks are nicely prebiotic and the yoghurt brings in some probiotics too.

4 tablespoons olive oil

4 leeks, washed and finely diced (discard any tough parts)

Few pinches of sea salt

Large handful of mint leaves, finely chopped

2 teaspoons Turkish dried chilli flakes (pul biber), plus extra to serve

1–2 pinches of hot dried chilli flakes, plus extra to serve

800ml (26fl oz) Bone Broth (ideally chicken) or Vegetable Broth (see pages 53–54)

Small bunch of dill (about 20g/¾oz), finely chopped

400g (14oz) live natural yoghurt

8 teaspoons warm Smoky Caramelised Butter (see page 227)

Large handful of Spicy Crunchy Chickpeas (see page 221)

Heat the olive oil very gently in a large pan, then add the leeks, salt, mint and both types of chilli flakes and cook gently for about 25 minutes, stirring often, until the leeks are soft and sweet.

Add the bone broth and dill to the leeks and bring to the boil, then take the pan off the heat and stir in 300g (11oz) of the yoghurt until well combined. There is no need to reheat the soup at this stage, but if you want to, reheat it gently to serving temperature but do not let it boil, otherwise the yoghurt will split.

Spoon a little of the liquid into the remaining yoghurt, so that it is runny enough to swirl onto the soup. Ladle the soup into bowls and swirl the remaining yoghurt on top, then drizzle 2 teaspoons of warm smoky butter over each portion. Sprinkle with spicy crunchy chickpeas and some extra chilli flakes (either Turkish or hot ones).

Serve with toasted sourdough bread rubbed with a garlic clove and drizzled with olive oil, or to make the soup more of a meal, add some cooked brown rice or cooked black lentils to the soup when you add the bone broth and serve with a poached or fried egg on top.

COCONUT AND CAULIFLOWER SOUP WITH MUSSELS

Serves 4

Although its pale appearance might lead you to think otherwise, cauliflower is packed with antioxidant nutrients from sulphur to vitamin C, and may even help to lower levels of bad cholesterol as it binds with bile acids in the gut. In this soup, cauliflower provides a prebiotic supporting role for a fragrant coconut broth and some juicy mussels – all doing a fantastic job of supporting gut and immune function. Quick to make and ridiculously delicious, it also works well with colourful varieties such as Romanesco or purple graffiti cauliflower.

1kg (2¼lb) fresh or frozen mussels in their shells

8 spring onions, green parts roughly chopped, white parts sliced and reserved

Bunch of coriander, stalks roughly chopped and leaves reserved

4 garlic cloves, roughly chopped

4 sticks of lemon grass, roughly chopped

40g (1½oz) fresh turmeric root, sliced into coins (optional, but don't use dried turmeric powder)

60g (2¼oz) fresh root ginger, sliced into coins

800ml (26fl oz) coconut milk

4–6 pinches of dried chilli flakes, plus extra to serve

4 teaspoons fish sauce (nam pla)

1 cauliflower, trimmed and cut into smallish florets

8 fresh chestnut or shiitake mushrooms, sliced

1 large romano pepper, de-seeded and sliced into rings

Juice of 1–2 limes

If you are using frozen mussels, simply defrost them in cool water while you make the soup. For fresh mussels, put them into a bowl of cold water, pull off any beardy bits and squeeze any that are open to see if they will close – discard any that remain open.

Put the green spring onion parts, the coriander stalks, garlic, lemon grass, turmeric root and ginger into a large pan. Add the coconut milk, chilli flakes, fish sauce and 500ml (18fl oz) of water. Bring to the boil, then cover, turn the heat down and simmer gently for 15–20 minutes, until the broth has taken on the flavours of the aromatics and is primrose yellow.

Strain the liquid through a sieve into a bowl, discard the aromatics, if you like, then return the broth to the pan and bring back to a simmer. Add the cauliflower to the broth and cook until tender, about 5 minutes. Fish out three-quarters of the cauliflower and set aside while you let the broth cool down for 10 minutes.

Pour the broth into a blender and blend until completely smooth (or blend with a stick blender). Return to the pan, bring back to a simmer, then add the reserved cauliflower, the mushrooms, white spring onion parts, romano pepper and mussels. Cover, bring to the boil, then simmer for a few minutes more until all the mussels are open and cooked through. Discard any that have not opened. Off the heat, add about 2 tablespoons of lime juice, to your taste.

Ladle the soup into four large soup bowls. Scatter with the reserved coriander leaves and some chilli flakes. Put a large bowl on the table for the mussel shells.

CAVOLO NERO AND CANNELLINI BEAN SOUP

Serves 4

My version of the Italian soup, Ribollita, is a proper meal in a bowl – savoury, sustaining and comforting at the end of a long day. It's even better a day or two later when the flavours have got cosy. Tinned beans are fine here, although you can soak, cook and freeze beans for convenience too. If you don't have cannellini, flageolet, haricot and borlotti beans all work well too. With outstanding members of the onion and cabbage family in addition to beans, this soup will keep your microbes very well fed indeed.

225g (8oz) dried cannellini beans or 2 x 400g (14oz) tins cannellini beans, rinsed and drained

4 tablespoons olive oil

3 large carrots, finely diced

3 large celery sticks, finely diced

1 red onion, finely diced

3 garlic cloves, very finely minced

1 heaped teaspoon fennel seeds

2 tablespoons tomato purée

200g (7oz) cavolo nero, washed and roughly chopped

1 litre (1¾ pints) chicken or pork Bone Broth (see page 53)

125g (4½oz) sourdough bread, torn up

Sea salt and freshly ground black pepper

Lemon wedges, to serve

If you are using dried beans, soak the beans overnight in plenty of cold water. Drain the soaked beans, then put into a pan and cover with fresh cold water. Bring to the boil and boil rapidly for 15 minutes, skimming off any froth that rises. Drain and rinse, return to the pan, cover with fresh water and bring to the boil again, then cover and simmer until tender but not collapsing, about 45–60 minutes. Drain, then set aside.

Meanwhile, heat the olive oil in a separate pan, add the carrots, celery, red onion, garlic and fennel seeds and sauté gently for about 30 minutes, until the veg are completely soft, sweet smelling and just starting to catch. Don't be tempted to hurry this bit. Add the tomato purée and cook, stirring for a few minutes more, until the tomato scent rises from the pan. Add the diced cavolo nero stalks, the cooked beans and bone broth, cover and simmer for another 30 minutes, stirring occasionally.

When the time is up, add the chopped cavolo nero leaves and bread to the pan, season with salt and pepper, add enough water to loosen the soup and simmer for another 5–10 minutes, until the cavolo nero is just tender. Ladle into bowls and serve each portion with a lemon wedge for people to squeeze over their soup.

JERUSALEM ARTICHOKE SOUP WITH TOASTED ALMONDS

Serves 4

Delicious Jerusalem artichokes are so famous for making you windy that we call them fartichokes and revert to being school children every time they are on the menu. They contain lots of prebiotic inulin, which may be broken down rather enthusiastically by your resident microbes. Long, slow cooking converts some of the inulin to fructose, resulting in sweet, creamy roots and less toots, but they are definitely a food for those who are confident about their digestive capacity!

80g (3oz) salted butter

2 onions, finely diced

4 celery sticks, finely diced

2 bay leaves

400g (14oz) Jerusalem artichokes (peeled weight)

450g (1lb) floury potatoes, peeled and diced

15g (½oz) herb fennel or dill fronds, finely chopped

180g (6oz) live natural yoghurt

4 teaspoons fresh lemon juice

Few pinches of sea salt

40g (1½oz) flaked almonds

Small handful of chives, finely snipped

Melt the butter in a pan over a medium heat, then sauté the onions and celery with the bay leaves for about 20 minutes, until everything is soft, sweet smelling and deeply golden.

Peel the Jerusalem artichokes and put them straight into acidulated water (you can do this by adding a squeeze of lemon juice or a dash of vinegar). Once they are all peeled, drain and dice, then add them to the pan with the potatoes and 1.2 litres (2 pints) of water. Bring to the boil, then cover and simmer for about 45 minutes, until the artichokes are soft enough to squash. Set aside for 10 minutes to cool slightly while you make the garnish.

Put the herb fennel or dill fronds into a blender with the yoghurt, lemon juice and salt, blitz until the yoghurt turns a little green and then pour into a bowl. Wash the blender. Toast the flaked almonds in a dry frying pan over a low heat for a few minutes, until they are just kissed with gold, then cool.

Pour the slightly cooled soup into the blender (fish out the bay leaves first) and blitz until it is velvety smooth. Check for salt and then return to the pan to gently heat through. Ladle into bowls and serve each portion topped with a swirl of the yoghurt, some toasted almonds and chives.

As this soup tastes rich and sweet, some bitter leaves and cold meat or goats' cheese make a great accompaniment.

BLACK BEAN SOUP

Serves 4

Black beans have a fudgy texture and fruity depth to their flavour. Slow-cooked pork hock (shin) makes the soup rich and velvety, smoky with chipotle and warm with cumin. This is proper peasant food; a good cheap meal that feels really meaty and sustaining, even though you only get a small amount of pork with each portion.

400g (14oz) dried black beans or 2 x 400g (14oz) tins black beans, rinsed and drained

1 tablespoon chicken, duck or bacon fat or lard

2 onions, finely chopped

1 large celery stick, finely chopped

350g (12oz) red peppers (ideally romano), de-seeded and roughly chopped

4–5 garlic cloves, finely chopped

1 heaped teaspoon cumin seeds

2 bay leaves

1 small pork hock (or 800g/1¾lb pork ribs or 2 trotters)

1 teaspoon smoked chipotle pepper (or hot smoked paprika)

1 tablespoon paprika

1 litre (1¾ pints) boiling water

1 tablespoon cider vinegar or sherry vinegar

Sea salt

TO SERVE

4 tablespoons crème fraîche (or soured cream or live natural yoghurt)

2 large handfuls of cherry tomatoes, quartered

Very large handful of coriander leaves

If you are using dried black beans, soak the beans overnight in plenty of cold water. Drain and rinse the soaked beans, then put into a pan and cover with fresh cold water. Bring to the boil and boil rapidly for 15 minutes, skimming off any froth that rises. Drain and rinse again, then set aside.

Melt the fat in a large pan, add the chopped vegetables, garlic, cumin seeds, bay leaves and pork hock and sauté gently for at least 20 minutes, stirring occasionally, until the onions are soft, sweet and caramelised. Add the chipotle pepper, paprika, black beans and boiling water and bring to the boil, then cover and simmer for 2½–3 hours, until the beans are collapsing and the meat is falling off the bone. Leave the lid off for a bit towards the end if the soup looks a bit watery, or add water if it's too thick. Add the vinegar and season with salt. Take out the pork and shred the meat with a fork, then return this to the soup, with the skin, if you like. Discard the bay leaves.

Let down the crème fraîche with a little water, so that you can swirl it on top of the soup. To serve, ladle the soup into bowls and garnish each portion with a swirl of crème fraîche, some cherry tomatoes and a scatter of coriander leaves. Add some toasted sourdough rubbed with garlic and drizzled with olive oil or warm corn tortillas for hungrier souls.

The soup will keep for up to 3 days in the fridge, or you can freeze leftovers for up to 3 months (simply defrost and reheat thoroughly before serving).

SALADS & VEGETABLES

HONEYED PEACH AND DANDELION SALAD WITH TOASTED HAZELNUTS

BLACK RICE SALAD WITH PINE NUTS AND PRESERVED LEMON

GRIDDLED ASPARAGUS WITH SIMPLE HOLLANDAISE

SWEET AND SPICY CAVOLO NERO

PURPLE SPROUTING BROCCOLI WITH GOMASIO

GREEN BEANS, ROAST BEETS, LABNEH AND CARAMELISED BUTTER

SALSIFY WITH TOAST HAZELNUTS AND CRÈME FRAÎCHE

MATCHSTICK SALAD

KIMCHI AND QUINOA SALAD

CREAMY HUMMUS WITH ROAST CARROTS AND CHERRY TOMATOES

GLOBE ARTICHOKES WITH ELDERFLOWER BUTTER

GREEN POTATO SALAD

A TOASTY NUTTY SALAD WITH RAW ARTICHOKE

All vegetables are heroes in my book, but here are some dishes that feature some of the superstars of gut-friendly food: salsify, artichokes, dandelions and asparagus amongst others. Rich with all types of fibre, resistant starch, enzymes, antioxidants and anti-inflammatory fats, this is just the starting point for your love affair with vegetables.

Although you might think that purple carrots are only for foodies, it's important to eat as many different varieties as you can lay your hands on, so if you see a bunch of purple carrots, a knobbly kohlrabi or some new salad greens, snap them up, because the chances are there's a microbe in your gut waiting patiently that will bloom and grow as a result. If you don't know what to do with new varieties, try roasting them in duck fat, or steaming and buttering them.

HONEYED PEACH AND DANDELION SALAD WITH TOASTED HAZELNUTS

Serves 4

Dandelion leaves support the liver and the young ones are just bitter enough to do the job without making you wince. Paired with succulent peaches, toasty hazelnuts, sweet fennel and a honey dressing, that bitterness gives a welcome kick to the whole thing. Dandelion leaves are also a good source of prebiotic inulin – feeding the good bacteria and keeping you satisfied for longer. Eat this salad to start your meal or to accompany some roast meat.

100g (4oz) hazelnuts

Juice of 1 lemon

1 tablespoon raw honey

90ml (3¼fl oz) olive oil

1 organic egg yolk (optional)

2 pinches of sea salt

4 large handfuls of small dandelion leaves, rinsed and dried

4 ripe peaches or nectarines, stoned and sliced

½ bunch of chives (about 30 stems), snipped into finger-sized lengths

20 herb fennel fronds

8–10 chive flowers

Toast the hazelnuts in a dry frying pan over a low heat for 15–20 minutes, moving the nuts around constantly to prevent burning. Tip them out onto a plate and leave to cool. Put the cooled hazelnuts into a clean tea towel and rub the skins off, then chop roughly.

Put the lemon juice into a small, lidded jar with the honey, olive oil, egg yolk and salt. Put the lid on securely and shake vigorously until emulsified and creamy. Set aside.

Arrange the dandelion leaves, peach or nectarine slices, chives and fennel fronds on dinner plates (try to get a little height on each plate). Scatter over the chopped hazelnuts, then pull the florets from the chive flowers, scattering these over, too. Spoon the dressing over and serve immediately before the leaves wilt.

BLACK RICE SALAD WITH PINE NUTS AND PRESERVED LEMON

Serves 6

Italian black rice is packed with antioxidants and it has a rich, nutty flavour and satisfying chew. Preserved lemon, red onion and roast carrots stud the deep purple of the rice, and a generous handful of raisins and barberries make each mouthful a perfect balance of sweet, sour, salty and savoury. When you eat rice cold, you benefit from the resistant starch that has formed as the rice chills, keeping your microbes happy and well fed.

300g (11oz) black rice (also called venus rice, riso nerone or riso venere)

2 teaspoons duck or bacon fat or other heat-stable fat

500g (1lb 2oz) carrots, sliced diagonally into 1cm (½in) pieces

100g (4oz) pine nuts

1 red onion, halved and sliced into thin half moons

100g (4oz) raisins

50g (2oz) dried barberries (or tart currants or dried cherries)

120g (4½oz) Preserved Lemon (see page 203), rind only, chopped

Finely grated zest and juice of 1 lemon

100ml (3½fl oz) extra-virgin olive oil

Freshly ground black pepper

Head of elderflowers or handful of thyme flowers, to finish (optional)

Rinse the black rice well, then drain and put into a large lidded pan with 600ml (1 pint) water. Bring to the boil, cover and simmer gently until all the water is absorbed, about 30–40 minutes. Turn off the heat, but leave the lid on for another 5 minutes, before tipping the rice onto a plate to cool. When cool enough, chill completely in the fridge for at least an hour.

Preheat the oven to 220°C/200°C fan/gas 7. Heat the fat in a frying pan and add the carrots, turning them over to completely cover in the fat. Tip onto a baking sheet and roast for 30–40 minutes, until sweet and soft with colour at the edges. Set aside to cool.

Meanwhile, lightly toast the pine nuts in a dry frying pan over a medium heat for about 3–4 minutes, then set aside to cool. Put the red onion slices into a bowl, cover with tepid water and leave for 3–4 minutes. Drain and rinse well with cold water, then drain again and tip into a large mixing bowl. Add the chilled rice, raisins, barberries, three-quarters of the preserved lemon rind, three-quarters of the pine nuts and the lemon zest to the bowl. Slice the carrots into slivers and add most of these, reserving just a few for garnish.

Make a dressing by shaking the lemon juice with the olive oil in a lidded jar until emulsified, then pour this over the salad. Mix everything well and taste for seasoning – it shouldn't need any salt, but add a few grinds of black pepper, and you may like to add the remaining preserved lemon rind, too.

Pile into a gorgeous bowl, or serve individually. Scatter the top of the salad with the reserved pine nuts and carrots and any edible flowers you have, if you like (simply flick the flowers from an elderflower head using the tines of a fork). Serve immediately or keep any leftovers in the fridge and eat within 48 hours of cooking the rice.

GRIDDLED ASPARAGUS WITH SIMPLE HOLLANDAISE

Serves 4

I can hardly think of a more delicious way to get your soluble fibre than a plate of asparagus and creamy hollandaise; when asparagus is in season, eat it as often as your wallet allows! Griddling asparagus retains a nice bit of bite and gives a smoky sweetness to the charred bits. You could do this on the barbecue if you don't have a griddle pan. Don't be scared of hollandaise, it just needs a little patience, and when made with organic eggs and butter, provides some nourishing fats in a soothing creamy form.

100g (4oz) unsalted butter

2 large organic egg yolks

Juice of 1 lemon

½ teaspoon white wine vinegar or sherry vinegar

½ teaspoon English mustard

Pinch of cayenne pepper, plus extra to serve

800g (1¾lb) asparagus spears

Sea salt

Melt the butter in a small pan, then transfer to a jug to cool a little. Put the egg yolks, 1 tablespoon of the lemon juice, the vinegar, mustard and cayenne into a heatproof bowl over a pan of gently simmering water and stir very slowly with a whisk to combine – don't beat it at any point or it can split. Stir like this until the egg yolks start to thicken a little and then start to pour in the melted butter in a very thin stream, stirring constantly. Start slowly with the butter, as this is the point it can split, and keep the heat as low as possible to avoid the eggs curdling.

When all the butter is in, turn the heat off under the pan, season with salt and add some more lemon juice to thin the sauce a little – it should taste lemony, but not sharp. If it is too thick to pour, stir in a little cool water to loosen it. Leave the bowl on the pan of hot water to keep warm and stir occasionally while you get on with griddling the asparagus.

Preheat a griddle pan over a highish heat until hot. Griddle the asparagus in batches for a few minutes on each side, until they have nice char marks on them. They should still have some bite to them.

Serve the griddled asparagus with the hollandaise drizzled over and an extra pinch of cayenne pepper sprinkled over, or put the sauce in a jug for people to help themselves.

SWEET AND SPICY CAVOLO NERO

Serves 4

Kale is a veritable powerhouse of nutrients and gut-friendly soluble fibre – it's not for nothing that your mother told you to eat your greens! The dark earthy flavour of cavolo nero is a perfect backdrop for a warmly spiced cumin and honey dressing and some sweet red onions.

2 red onions, halved and sliced into thin half moons

Handful of pumpkin seeds

2 teaspoons cumin seeds

2 pinches of sea salt

4 pinches of chilli powder

2 teaspoons raw honey

4 teaspoons fresh lemon juice

4 teaspoons extra-virgin olive oil

300g (11oz) cavolo nero or kale, washed and sliced

Put the red onions into a bowl, cover with warm water, leave for 3–4 minutes, then drain and rinse well with cold water. Leave to drain.

Toast the pumpkin seeds in a dry frying pan over a high heat, moving them constantly, until they start to pop and smell nutty. Set aside to cool.

To make the dressing, first toast the cumin seeds in a dry frying pan over a medium heat for a few minutes, until they smell aromatic, then tip into a pestle and mortar with the salt and coarsely grind. Put into a lidded jar with the chilli powder, honey, lemon juice and olive oil. Tightly close the lid, shake well and taste for salt, lemon or chilli heat.

Put a steamer on the stove and steam the cavolo nero or kale for about 3–4 minutes, until the stalks are al dente, then tip into a bowl with the blanched onions. Pour over the dressing and toss, then scatter with the toasted pumpkin seeds. Eat warm or at room temperature.

PURPLE SPROUTING BROCCOLI WITH GOMASIO

Serves 4

Purple sprouting broccoli is as good as asparagus in my opinion and particularly delicious dipped first into a garlicky sauce and then tasty, savoury gomasio. The sauce is also great with sweet potato wedges, roast vegetables and simple grain salads alike. Make extra and it will keep in the fridge for a few days if you can resist it that long. Needless to say, the combination of broccoli, garlic, raw honey and olive oil will keep your microbes as happy as your taste buds.

4 garlic cloves

3–4 pinches of sea salt

4 pinches of dried chilli flakes

2 teaspoons raw honey

1–2 tablespoons fresh lemon juice

2 tablespoons olive oil

300g (11oz) purple-sprouting broccoli, trimmed

Gomasio (see page 214), to serve

Crush the garlic into a paste with the salt – I use the flat side of a large knife or a pestle and mortar. Put the garlic paste into a mixing bowl with the chilli flakes, honey and a tablespoon of the lemon juice and whisk to combine. Add the olive oil, a little at a time, whisking well between each addition to emulsify the sauce, or shake the sauce in a small jar with a lid. Taste for lemon and add more if you think it needs it. The sauce should be lemony but not sour and the texture creamy – too much lemon juice will make it split. Set aside.

Put a steamer on the stove and steam the broccoli for a few minutes, until the stalks are al dente.

Divide the broccoli between four plates and let everyone help themselves to a puddle of sauce and a pile of gomasio. Dip the broccoli first into the sauce and then into the gomasio.

GREEN BEANS, ROAST BEETS, LABNEH AND CARAMELISED BUTTER

Serves 4

This cooked salad has a little bit of everything, roasty, sweet, creamy, spicy, crisp and the indefinably moreish quality of caramelised butter. Crunchy chickpeas, beets, onions and pistachios raise the fibre content of this dish in the most elegant way, and nigella seeds are said to calm the antisocial side effects of too many pulses.

300g (11oz) raw beetroots

Olive oil, for drizzling

Couple of pinches of sea salt

300g (11oz) green beans

1 small red onion, halved, then thinly sliced

150g (5oz) Labneh (see page 210)

1 x quantity Spicy Crunchy Chickpeas recipe (see page 221)

50g (2oz) raw pistachio nuts, lightly crushed

1 teaspoon nigella seeds

2 tablespoons Caramelised Butter (see page 227)

½ lemon, quartered

Preheat the oven to 180°C/160°C fan/gas 4. Scrub the beetroots and trim off any really rough bits of skin, slice into quarters (or more if large) and put into a mixing bowl. Drizzle with a little olive oil, sprinkle over the salt, turn to coat and then tip onto a baking sheet. Roast for about an hour until tender to the point of a knife. Set aside to cool until just warm.

Steam the green beans until just tender, refresh under cold water, then drain and pile onto a large serving plate. Cover the red onion slices in tepid water for a few minutes, then drain and refresh in cold water. Scatter them over the green beans. Cut the beetroot quarters in half, scatter over the plate and place rough pieces of labneh over the vegetables. If you have time, leave the salad for 10 minutes for the beet colour to bleed into the labneh.

Scatter the crunchy chickpeas, crushed pistachios and nigella seeds over the salad just before you eat. Drizzle with warm caramelised butter and nestle the pieces of lemon into the salad.

Eat with Teff and Sesame Pancakes (see page 122) or flatbread, Broad Bean Hummus (see page 120) and steamed greens or a salad of bitter greens.

SALSIFY WITH TOASTED HAZELNUTS AND CRÈME FRAÎCHE

Serves 4

Salsify or scorzonera is a strange-looking relative of the dandelion, all gnarly and blackened outside, but pearl white inside with a delicate flavour reminiscent of artichokes and green hazelnuts. It's called the vegetable oyster, but I can't detect any sea flavours at all; I see it as more of an elegant cousin of the parsnip, with less sweetness and more complexity. Rich with soluble fibre, it makes a satisfying accompaniment for dark greens, fish dishes and roast dinners.

150g (5oz) hazelnuts

Good squeeze of fresh lemon juice or splash of white wine vinegar

600g (1lb 5oz) salsify or scorzonera roots

180g (6oz) crème fraîche

2 good pinches of sea salt

Freshly ground black pepper

Toast the hazelnuts in a dry frying pan over a low heat until the skins start to fall off and they are tinged all over with gold, about 15–20 minutes. Set aside to cool.

Have ready a bowl of water with the lemon juice or vinegar added. Scrub and peel the salsify, then slice on the slant into long coins, dropping these into the acidulated water as you go. When it's all prepared, drain the sliced salsify and steam for 10–12 minutes, until tender. If salsify is undercooked it turns grey as it cools.

While the salsify steams, tip the hazelnuts into a clean tea towel and rub the skins off. Tip out onto a baking tray, step outside and blow the skins away as you shake the tray. Yes, your neighbours will wonder what you are doing. Chop the hazelnuts so that most are very finely chopped, but a few are left almost whole, then set aside for a moment.

When the salsify is ready, put it into a mixing bowl with the crème fraîche, three-quarters of the hazelnuts, the salt and lots of black pepper – you want to feel a little heat from the pepper. Turn everything over to coat and then serve, sprinkled with the remaining hazelnuts.

This works well served both hot and at room temperature, but the crème fraîche will set if you chill it in the fridge, so you may need to warm leftovers through a little before serving. It will keep in an airtight container in the fridge for up to 2 days.

MATCHSTICK SALAD

Serves 4

Crisp raw celeriac has a fresh celery flavour and is far more prebiotic than when cooked, but not much fun to chew through when crudely chopped. The secret is to slice it into thin matchstick pieces that soften after a little time spent mingling with lemon juice and beet kvass. The kvass turns the salad an intense shade of fuchsia pink that I particularly love – if you prefer, leave out the kvass and use extra lemon juice for a classy blonde version. Serve as a side for rich meats or fish dishes, or scatter over a breakfast veg bowl.

200ml (7fl oz) Beet Kvass (see page 244)

Juice of 1 lemon

2 teaspoons raw honey

6 pinches of sea salt

1 celeriac root

1 red onion, halved and sliced into very thin half moons (or a bunch of spring onions, sliced)

2 heaped teaspoons cumin seeds

Put the beet kvass, lemon juice, honey and salt into a mixing bowl and stir until the honey dissolves.

Peel the celeriac root and slice in half. Lay the flat side of one half on a chopping board and slice into 2–3mm (1/16–1/8in) thick slices, or do this on a mandolin. Pile up a few slices of celeriac and slice through them to make matchstick-sized pieces, about 5cm (2in) long by 2–3mm (1/16–1/8in) wide.

Put the matchsticks into the mixing bowl with the kvass dressing and turn to coat. Repeat until all the celeriac is used up and you have a bowl of pink, lemony matchsticks. Add the red onion slices and mix well.

Cover the bowl and chill in the fridge for at least an hour – a few hours is better, as the celeriac will soften as it sits.

When you are ready to serve, toast the cumin seeds in a dry frying pan over a medium heat until they start to smell aromatic, about 3–4 minutes. Tip into the celeriac mixture and stir well.

The salad will keep in an airtight container in the fridge for at least 3 days.

KIMCHI AND QUINOA SALAD

Serves 4

This zingy probiotic salad is a doddle to put together once you have made yourself a delicious jar of Kimchi (see page 198). It also works with milder Sunshine Sauerkraut (see page 202) or Ribbon Pickle (see page 209) for a lower FODMAP option. I keep precooked quinoa in the freezer, packed flat in freezer bags, so that I can throw this salad together in minutes. To make it a more substantial meal, add some shredded cooked meat or fish, or a couple of soft-boiled eggs, some fried tempeh or a handful of cooked adzuki or black beans.

400g (14oz) cooked quinoa or 175g (6oz) dry weight quinoa

8 chestnut mushrooms or large button mushrooms, sliced

200g (7oz) pink radishes or breakfast radishes, thinly sliced

2 handfuls of coriander leaves

300g (11oz) Kimchi (see page 198)

Cold-pressed sesame oil, or sunflower oil for drizzling

4 handfuls of soft salad leaves (about 100g/4oz), rinsed and patted dry

If you don't have precooked quinoa, cover the dry quinoa in cold water and leave to soak for 6–12 hours at room temperature. Rinse through a sieve until there is no soapy froth, then drain and put into a lidded pan with 175g (6oz) water. Bring to the boil, cover, then turn the heat down and simmer until the water is all absorbed, about 10 minutes. Check to see if it's ready by pulling back the quinoa to see the bottom of the pan. Turn off the heat but leave the lid on the pan for another 5 minutes and then tip the quinoa out onto a plate to cool. It's worth cooking larger amounts and storing in the freezer (just use from frozen as it will defrost quickly).

Put three-quarters of the mushrooms and radishes into a mixing bowl and reserve the remainder. Add three-quarters of the coriander leaves, the quinoa and most of the kimchi to the bowl, drizzle in a good glug of sesame oil and mix well. If you are using cooked pulses, add these now. Check for seasoning – you shouldn't need any salt or lemon as the kimchi is salty and sour, but you might want to add more oil.

Put a handful of salad leaves into each of four large dining bowls and top with the quinoa salad. Arrange the remaining mushrooms, radishes, kimchi and coriander leaves on top and add any protein that you are using.

CREAMY HUMMUS WITH ROAST CARROTS AND CHERRY TOMATOES

Serves 4

Flageolet beans are the siblings of haricot beans, picked when still tender and slightly green. For a pulse, they are easy to digest and make the creamiest hummus; a perfect foil here for sweet roast vegetables. This is a dish that is so easy to prepare, but feels much more complex and looks impressive.

2 tablespoons plus 1 teaspoon duck, chicken, goose or bacon fat or coconut oil

1kg (2¼lb) carrots, left whole if small, or cut into chunky batons

2 red onions, each cut into 8 wedges

2 teaspoons fennel seeds

2 teaspoons nigella seeds

350g (12oz) cherry vine tomatoes

2 garlic cloves, finely chopped

500g (1lb 2oz) cooked flageolet beans (most of 2 x 400g/14oz tins, rinsed and drained, or 250g/9oz dried weight)

4 tablespoons tahini

4 tablespoons cold-pressed sunflower or rapeseed oil

1–2 teaspoons sea salt, plus extra for seasoning

Juice of 1–2 lemons

Handful of flat-leaf parsley, leaves picked

Extra-virgin olive oil, for drizzling

Preheat the oven to 200°C/180°C fan/gas 6. Put the 2 tablespoons of fat into a roasting tray and melt in the oven for a few minutes, then add the carrots and red onions and toss to coat. Sprinkle with a little salt and the fennel and nigella seeds. Roast for about 45 minutes, until soft and a little caramelised at the edges. After about 25 minutes, put the cherry tomatoes, still on their vines, onto another roasting tray greased with the remaining 1 teaspoon of fat and roast these for about 20 minutes, until the skins split and they smell sweet.

Make the hummus while the vegetables roast. Mash the garlic into a paste with a pinch of salt, using the flat side of a large knife. Put the garlic paste, flageolet beans, tahini, sunflower or rapeseed oil, 1 teaspoon of the salt and the juice of 1 lemon into the jug of a blender and whizz until the mixture is creamy and smooth. Taste and decide whether you think it needs more salt or lemon – it probably will. Gradually add 50–75ml (2–3fl oz) of water and blend again between additions until you have a smooth, creamy paste with the texture of whipped cream.

Spread the hummus over a large serving plate, scatter with parsley leaves and drizzle with olive oil. As soon as the roast vegetables are ready, scatter these over the hummus and tuck in. Some warm whole grain pitta bread (or Teff and Sesame Pancakes, see page 122) and a crisp green salad are great accompaniments.

GLOBE ARTICHOKES WITH ELDERFLOWER BUTTER

Serves 4

Globe artichokes might look a little scary to the uninitiated, related as they are to thistles, but they are sweetly subtle and intriguingly delicious. I urge you to ignore all that guff about fancy preparation and simply boil them, pull the leaves off at the table and dip them into something tart and creamy, for the simplest starter ever. Crème fraîche with black pepper, Hollandaise (see page 144) or a simple olive oil and lemon dressing all work well if you can't find elderflowers.

All members of the thistle family support the liver and contain masses of prebiotic fibre.

4 globe artichokes
40g (1½oz) salted butter
2 unblemished elderflower heads
Pinch of sea salt
1 tablespoon fresh lemon juice

Put the artichokes into a pan and cover with boiling water. Bring back to the boil, cover with a lid and simmer for 20–30 minutes, until one of the leaves easily pulls away from the body. Drain and set aside to cool a little while you make the butter.

Melt the butter in a small pan, then take off the heat and immerse the elderflower heads in it for a minute or so – just the flower parts. Squeeze the butter out of the flower heads into the pan using clean hands, then discard the elderflowers. Whisk the salt and lemon juice into the butter until it is velvety smooth, then pour into a little jug, or give everyone a tiny ramekin or shot glass of it.

Put a large bowl in the centre of the table for everyone to discard their leaves and chokes into. To eat the artichoke, peel off the leaves, starting at the base and working your way towards the centre. Dip the base of each leaf into the elderflower butter and scrape off the soft artichoke meat with your teeth. As the leaves get near the centre they will be too soft to do this with, so pull them all off to reveal the thistly inner choke. This is absolutely not edible, so scrape it all out using a teaspoon and then eat the delicious artichoke heart you have revealed. The whole process is a wonderful way of slowing down, and perfect if you are apt to bolt your food.

GREEN POTATO SALAD

Serves 4

Cold potatoes are an excellent source of resistant starch; in fact, eating them this way means that you convert much less of the carbohydrate to glucose, avoiding a rise in blood sugar. This salad is vividly green with so many herbs running through it you can feel it soothing your immune system with every bite. Parsley is a great source of vitamin C throughout the winter, so don't just make this when the sun is shining.

100g (4oz) frozen peas

750g (1lb 10oz) waxy salad potatoes, boiled, cooled and chilled for at least 3 hours

4–5 spring onions, sliced (or 1 shallot, sliced)

60g (2¼oz) parsley, basil or wild garlic leaves

1–2 garlic cloves

100ml (3½fl oz) extra-virgin olive oil

Juice of ½ lemon

4–5 pinches of sea salt

1 teaspoon raw honey (optional)

Add the frozen peas to a pan of boiling water, bring back to the boil, then immediately tip into a colander and refresh with cold water. Drain well and put into a mixing bowl.

Break the cold potatoes into rough-edged pieces with your hands and add them to the mixing bowl along with the spring onions.

To make the dressing, put all the remaining ingredients into a blender and blend until completely smooth. Taste and adjust the seasoning with a little more lemon juice and honey (if using), or add more oil if you think it is not smooth enough. Pour the dressing over the vegetables and turn to coat.

This salad will keep (covered) in the fridge for at least 24 hours, but the herbs won't taste quite as fresh.

A TOASTY NUTTY SALAD WITH RAW ARTICHOKE

Serves 4

Raw Jerusalem artichoke is crisp, sweet and nutty – rather like a water chestnut with more flavour. Bursting with prebiotic inulin, it is sure to give your microbes a feast! Because they are so prebiotic when raw, they can cause something of a carnival in your colon, depending on your microbial make-up and the frequency that you eat inulin-containing foods. Luckily this salad is delicious with or without the artichoke, so you can decide how much or how little to add.

12 rashers streaky bacon

1 tablespoon duck, goose, bacon or chicken fat

4 slices of sourdough bread, roughly torn into croûton-sized chunks

100g (4oz) walnuts

2–3 firm young Jerusalem artichokes

Juice of ½ lemon

1–2 teaspoons raw honey

1 x quantity Velvet Dressing recipe (see page 226) made with cold-pressed sunflower oil

120g (4½oz) rocket leaves, rinsed and patted dry

80g (3oz) watercress leaves

200g (7oz) ripe goats' cheese or ripe Brie

Cook the bacon very slowly in a dry frying pan over a low heat until crisp all over, about 10–12 minutes. Set aside when it's ready, but don't wash the pan.

Melt the duck (or other) fat in the bacon pan, add the bread chunks and fry gently until golden brown on all sides, about 5 minutes, then set aside to cool on kitchen paper.

Toast the walnuts in another frying pan over a low heat, moving the nuts around frequently to prevent burning. When the skins are starting to crack and the nuts are touched with golden brown, about 15 minutes, tip into a clean tea towel and rub as much of the skin off as you can. Set aside to cool.

Peel the artichokes and slice them into wafer-thin coins, preferably using a mandolin. Drop them straight into a bowl of cold water with the lemon juice added.

Add the honey to the dressing, so that it tastes mildly sweet. Put the rocket and watercress leaves into a mixing bowl and dress with half of the dressing, tossing to coat.

Divide the leaves between four plates, placing a mound on each. Scatter the toasted walnuts and croûtons over the leaves and dot with pieces of cheese. Drain the artichoke coins, scatter as many as you dare over the salad, then top with the crisp rashers of bacon and drizzle with the remaining dressing.

MEALS

TEFF BURRITOS WITH PULLED PORK AND PICKLES

LAMB KOFTAS WITH CREAMY CELERIAC AND SPRING ONIONS

RAMEN BOWL WITH CARAMELISED SWEET POTATO

SMOKED MACKEREL AND CUCUMBER NORI-MAKI

SIMPLE CLAM LAKSA WITH OMELETTE NOODLES

TACOS WITH VELVETY PINTO BEANS, SALSA AND CAJUN KRAUT

CRISPY LAMB WITH LEMONY FLAGEOLET BEANS AND ROAST TOMATOES

FRAGRANT RICE WITH SPICED ROAST SQUASH AND BLACK BEANS

CREAMY CHICKPEA POLENTA WITH MUSHROOMS AND CHICKEN LIVERS

SAGE AND ONION QUICHE WITH A CHESTNUT CRUST

BAKED COD WITH A PISTACHIO CRUST

SOOTHING DAL WITH PLUM CHUTNEY AND ROAST RADISHES

I'm a bit of a magpie when it comes to food, pinching ideas from around the globe and finding joy in a huge range of different flavours. I'll get a taste for something and want to eat it for days before I move onto my next flavour crush. Our bodies long for variety in all forms; flavour, seasonality and novelty excite our palates and give our microbes the variety they need to be strong and adaptive.

What makes a meal really sing for me is a contrast in texture; a salty crisp piece of lamb soothed by creamy flageolet beans, or sharp pickles against the softest pulled pork.

Many of the elements of these gut-friendly meals can be made ahead and stashed away in the fridge or freezer for weekday meals when you need quick sustenance that tastes as good as it looks.

TEFF BURRITOS WITH PULLED PORK AND PICKLES

Serves 4

Who could resist succulent pulled pork and a self-assembly meal full of mouth-watering pickles? These deeply savoury burritos are packed with prebiotic fibre that your gut will love, plus all the elements can be made ahead and frozen for a meal that comes together in minutes. Not all the pork will be eaten, but it is best to cook a decent amount at one go, especially as it only seems to improve over the next few days!

1.5kg (3lb 5oz) shoulder of pork on the bone

1 teaspoon fennel seeds

1 tablespoon sea salt, plus extra for seasoning

1 tablespoon dark muscovado sugar

2 teaspoons smoked paprika

TO SERVE

1 x quantity Teff and Sesame Pancakes recipe (see page 122)

1 cucumber, sliced into quarters lengthways and then into long diagonal pieces, about 3mm (⅛in) thick

Bunch of coriander, leaves picked

Juice of 2 limes

1 teaspoon raw honey

2–3 pinches dried chilli flakes

2 ripe avocados

Sunshine Sauerkraut or Kimchi (see pages 202 and 198)

Radish and Pomegranate Pickles (see page 207) (or fresh sliced radishes)

Salad leaves, rinsed and patted dry

First, cook your pork. Ideally, do this 24 hours in advance so the meat can develop flavour. Preheat the oven to 240°C/220°C fan/gas 9. Dry the meat with kitchen paper and line a roasting tray with foil, leaving enough overhang to wrap over the pork. Place the pork onto the foil. Grind the fennel seeds with the salt and then mix this with the sugar and smoked paprika before thoroughly rubbing into the pork. Roast the pork, uncovered, for 35–45 minutes, until golden brown.

Turn the oven down to 150°C/130°C fan/gas 2 and wrap the pork up securely in the foil. Roast for about 6 hours, until it is completely soft and pieces can be pulled away easily. Pour off the juices and reserve.

Turn the oven back up to 240°C/220°C fan/gas 9 and roast the pork, uncovered, for a further 10–15 minutes to crisp up. Once out of the oven, loosely cover with fresh foil and leave to rest for at least 30 minutes.

Pull the pork into shreds and add the meat juices from the tray. Taste and decide if you need any more salt or smoked paprika. If possible, leave to rest in the fridge for 24 hours, or freeze for up to 3 months.

When you are ready to eat, preheat the oven to 160°C/140°C fan/gas 3 and warm the teff pancakes and 400–500g (14oz–1lb 2oz) of the pulled pork in the oven (covered with foil) for about 15 minutes.

Put the cucumber and coriander leaves into a salad bowl with a few good pinches of salt, the lime juice and honey, then sprinkle in the chilli flakes and toss to combine. Taste and see if it needs more honey, chilli flakes or salt. Peel, stone and slice the avocados, then set this on the table with the cucumber salad, sunshine sauerkraut, radish and pomegranate pickles, salad leaves, and the warmed pork and teff pancakes.

Let everyone tuck in and load their own burritos.

LAMB KOFTAS WITH CREAMY CELERIAC AND SPRING ONIONS

Serves 4

These succulent lamb koftas have become one of my comfort meals. They are so satisfyingly rich that a small amount of meat is enough, allowing the vegetables to shine. Creamy, garlicky tahini sauce ties everything together and a pink tangle of rhubarb pickle gives a salty, sour kick that helps you digest the rich lamb.

FOR THE RHUBARB PICKLE
1 pink rhubarb stalk
Pinch of sea salt
1 heaped teaspoon raw honey (or 3 pinches of caster sugar)

FOR THE CELERIAC PURÉE
1 large celeriac, peeled and cut into rough chunks
4 tablespoons olive oil
2–3 pinches of sea salt
Freshly ground black pepper

FOR THE KOFTAS
1 teaspoon fennel seeds
1 teaspoon coriander seeds
½ teaspoon cumin seeds
Pinch of dried chilli flakes
3 pinches of sea salt
400g (14oz) lamb mince
Finely grated zest of 1 lemon
4 spring onions or 1 onion, finely chopped
2–3 teaspoons duck or goose fat, lard or dripping

First, make the rhubarb pickle. Cut the rhubarb in half lengthways and use a peeler to shave into long lengths. Lay the lengths next to each other and cut in half widthways. Alternatively, cut the rhubarb into thin wafers. Mix the rhubarb with the salt and honey and set aside for an hour, or chill in the fridge for up to 48 hours. If you don't have rhubarb, Kimchi (see page 198) or Ribbon Pickle (see page 209) makes a great alternative.

Next, make the celeriac purée. Steam the celeriac until very tender, about 15 minutes. Put into a blender with the olive oil, salt and lots of black pepper and blend until smooth. Keep warm.

While the celeriac cooks, make the koftas. Toast the fennel, coriander and cumin seeds in a dry frying pan over a medium heat for a few minutes until fragrant and then tip into a pestle and mortar. Add the chilli flakes and salt, grind the spices finely, then put into a mixing bowl with the lamb mince, lemon zest and onions, mixing everything well with your hands. Form the mixture into 20 balls and set aside until you are ready to cook them.

12 spring onions, trimmed (leaving most of the green part)

1kg (2¼lb) broad beans (weight with pods), podded

300g (11oz) purple-sprouting broccoli, trimmed

Tahini Sauce (see page 224), to serve

For the vegetables, heat a griddle pan or dry frying pan over a highish heat until hot, then scorch the spring onions on both sides, about 7–8 minutes. Set aside.

Put the steamer on for the vegetables (the veg and koftas will take about the same amount of time to cook).

Melt the fat of your choice in a frying pan and fry the koftas over a highish heat until colouring on the outside, but still squashy to pressure (they should be pink on the inside), about 3–4 minutes. Meanwhile, steam the broad beans and broccoli.

To serve, spread the celeriac purée on one side of each dinner plate and top with the koftas. Lay the purple sprouting broccoli and spring onions on the other side of the plate and scatter with broad beans. Place a tangle of rhubarb pickle to one side and drizzle with tahini sauce – or let people serve themselves (and give those that don't like tahini some olive oil and a lemon quarter).

RAMEN BOWL WITH CARAMELISED SWEET POTATO

Serves 4

A nourishing ramen bowl is all about balance; from the rich, salty broth, savoury tempeh and sweet arame seaweed to the pickled vegetables that perch on top, everything is chosen to promote harmony. I love to use naturally gluten-free shirataki noodles made from konjac – a root incredibly rich in gut-friendly soluble fibre and low in starch. Prepare everything in advance and you can put your ramen bowl together in a matter of minutes.

FOR THE BROTH

1 litre (1¾ pints) chicken Bone Broth or Vegetable Broth (see pages 53–54)

50g (2oz) fresh root ginger, sliced

4 garlic cloves, finely chopped

Thinly pared rind of 1 lemon

8 spring onions, green parts sliced (white parts reserved for later)

Pinch of dried chilli flakes

FOR THE RAMEN BOWL

30g (1¼oz) dried arame seaweed

7 teaspoons chicken or duck fat

250g (9oz) purple or orange sweet potato (or squash), peeled and cut into 15mm (⅝in) dice

2 pinches of dried chilli flakes, plus extra to serve

1 teaspoon tamari

225g (8oz) tempeh block, cut in half then into 1cm (½in) slices

8 fresh shiitake or chestnut mushrooms, thickly sliced

170g (6oz) shirataki noodles (the pre-soaked kind)

2 soft-boiled organic eggs (optional)

6–8 teaspoons genmai miso

4 pickled Radish Bombs (see page 208) or 12 pieces of pink pickled ginger, thinly sliced

Gomasio, Pickled Baby Courgettes and Shichimi Togarashi (see pages 214, 201 and 216), to serve

To make the broth, heat the bone broth in a large pan until just simmering. Add all the remaining broth ingredients and simmer for about 20 minutes, then strain out the bits and keep the broth warm.

Meanwhile, for the ramen bowl, cover the seaweed in cold water and leave to soak for 20–30 minutes, then rinse and drain. For the caramelised sweet potato, heat 2 teaspoons of the fat in a large frying pan, add the sweet potato and cook gently for about 15 minutes, shaking the pan occasionally, until the inside is soft and the outside crisp. Add the chilli flakes, sprinkle over the tamari and shake to coat. Once the tamari has evaporated, tip the sweet potato into a bowl and wash the pan so you can use it for the tempeh.

For the tempeh, melt 3 teaspoons of the remaining fat in the frying pan and fry the tempeh until golden on both sides, about 5 minutes. Put 3 tablespoons of water into a small bowl and add 8 shakes of tamari. Add the tamari water to the pan and cook, turning the tempeh over gently, until the liquid evaporates, about a minute. Set aside and wash the pan again.

For the mushrooms, melt the remaining fat in the frying pan, add the mushrooms and fry over a high heat until tinged golden, about 3–4 minutes, then add a few shakes of tamari to the pan and set aside.

Bring a small pan of water to the boil, add the shirataki noodles, bring back to the boil and then drain. Slice the reserved white parts of the spring onions and soft-boil your eggs, if you are adding these.

To assemble, divide the noodles between four bowls, top with the seaweed and scatter over the sweet potato. Stir the miso into the warm broth and then pour into the bowls. Arrange the tempeh, mushrooms, spring onions and pickled radish bombs or ginger slices over the top and nestle in a peeled boiled egg half (if using). Put some chilli flakes, gomasio, pickled baby courgettes and shichimi togarashi on the table for people to help themselves.

SMOKED MACKEREL AND CUCUMBER NORI-MAKI

Serves 4

Nori-maki are those lovely sushi rolls that are bound by a striking sheet of black nori seaweed. Sushi must be one of the most delicious ways to get some of the resistant starch that your gut microbes love to feast on. It's important to cool your rice in order to allow the resistant starch to form, so cook your rice at least a couple of hours in advance. I've chosen to replace fiery wasabi with a classic English mackerel accompaniment, hot horseradish sauce. It works brilliantly!

FOR THE SUSHI RICE

250g (9oz) sushi rice

4 teaspoons Japanese rice vinegar

2 pinches of sea salt

40g (1½oz) black sesame seeds

FOR THE NORI-MAKI

1 shallot, finely diced

2 tablespoons Japanese rice vinegar

4 sheets of dried nori seaweed, cut in half

8 teaspoons hot horseradish sauce

50g (2oz) boneless smoked mackerel, shredded

2–3 spring onions, very finely chopped

15cm (6in) piece of cucumber, halved, de-seeded and cut into long, thin strips

4 teaspoons fermented black soya beans or miso paste

For the rice, soak the sushi rice in cold water for 30 minutes, then drain and rinse. Put the soaked rice into a pan with 500ml (18fl oz) of water and bring to the boil, then cover and simmer until the water is absorbed, about 15–20 minutes. Take off the heat and leave in the covered pan for a further 10 minutes. Tip the rice into a bowl, mix in the rice vinegar, salt and sesame seeds, then leave to cool to room temperature. Chill for about 30 minutes in the fridge – not too long or the rice can start to harden up.

Assemble all your ingredients for the nori-maki so that you can have a little production line going. You will make four rolls of mackerel sushi and four of cucumber. Put the shallot into a bowl, cover with the rice vinegar and set aside.

Place a half sheet of nori on your sushi mat with the long side facing you and spread an eighth of the rice across it using the back of a teaspoon. Leave 1cm (½in) free of rice at the far side of the nori sheet. To make the mackerel nori-maki, spread a teaspoon of horseradish sauce in a line across the rice about a third of the way up from the bottom of the sheet. Place a quarter of the mackerel on top and nestle some spring onions alongside. Wet the rice-free strip of nori and the tip of your finger with water, then roll up tightly using the mat so that both edges of the nori meet and overlap slightly. Set aside while you make another three mackerel rolls.

To make the cucumber nori-maki, use the long cucumber strips in place of mackerel, use the vinegared shallot (drain it first) in place of spring onions, and spread a teaspoon of fermented black soya beans or miso paste next to the horseradish. When the rolls are all complete, use a very sharp knife to slice each roll into six pieces and serve with a big bowl of salad or some steamed greens and maybe a bowl of Miso Soup (see page 57).

SIMPLE CLAM LAKSA WITH OMELETTE NOODLES

Serves 4

A laksa is essentially a spicy south-east Asian noodle soup that can be either creamy or sour. Because I love a creamy soup and a bowlful of seashells to dig through hungrily, I make mine with clams and coconut milk. Prebiotic leek shreds and strips of rolled omelette take the place of more traditional white rice noodles, and the soup is topped with some fibre-rich black beans and asparagus (although out of season you could use sprouting broccoli, French beans or mangetout). The essential slow cook of the aromatics can be done in advance to make this a quick meal.

1 tablespoon coriander seeds

3 tablespoons coconut oil or duck fat, plus extra for greasing

20g (¾oz) peeled turmeric root, very finely chopped

200g (7oz) shallots, very finely chopped

30g (1¼oz) lemon grass (light parts only), very finely chopped

10g (¼oz) grated fresh root ginger

1½–2 teaspoons dried chilli flakes, plus extra to serve

4 organic eggs, well beaten

1½–2 tablespoons shrimp paste

800ml (26fl oz) coconut milk (unshaken)

4 leeks (white and pale parts only), washed and cut in half lengthways then into long shreds (like noodles!)

800g (1¾lb) clams (fresh or precooked in their shells)

400g (14oz) asparagus spears, woody parts snapped or cut off

150g (5oz) cooked black beans

Handful of Moroccan mint or laksa leaves, finely chopped

2 limes, each cut into quarters

Finely grind the coriander seeds using a pestle and mortar and set aside. Melt the coconut oil or duck fat in a large pan set over a low heat, add the turmeric root, shallots, lemon grass, ginger, ground coriander and 1½ teaspoons of the chilli flakes and cook gently, stirring occasionally, for at least 20 minutes. (This can be done up to 24 hours in advance and kept in the fridge.)

To make the omelette noodles, put a heavy-based frying pan over a highish heat, then use a wad of kitchen paper to carefully grease the pan with duck fat or lard. Pour in enough beaten egg to coat the bottom of the pan and cook the egg crêpe for about a minute, until it starts to curl at the edges, then tip it out onto a board. Repeat until all the beaten egg is used up. Roll up the crêpes and slice across each roll to make noodles. Set aside.

Add the shrimp paste to taste to the shallot mixture and cook for a minute, then add the coconut milk and bring to the boil. Add the leeks, cover and cook over a medium heat until they are just soft, about 7–8 minutes. Check for spiciness and add more chilli flakes, if you like.

If you are using fresh clams, soak them in cold water for 10 minutes, then discard any that do not close when tapped; for precooked, just defrost under cold running water in the bag.

Add the asparagus to the laksa and then the fresh clams. Cover and cook until the clams have all opened (discard any unopened ones) and the asparagus is al dente, about 3–4 minutes. Precooked clams just need to be reheated, so add them a couple of minutes later.

Divide the omelette noodles between four bowls. Remove the asparagus from the laksa, gently stir in the black beans and then ladle the laksa into the bowls. Top with the asparagus, mint or laksa leaves and a couple of lime quarters (per portion) for people to squeeze over their meal. Serve with extra chilli flakes for those who like it spicy, and a bowl for the shells.

TACOS WITH VELVETY PINTO BEANS, SALSA AND CAJUN KRAUT

Serves 4

The amusing poses that people strike as they try not to get salsa down their front can make tacos a relaxing and fun meal, but definitely not first-date fare. If you've ever had Tex-mex refried beans from a tin served in a crispy taco shell, prepare to be amazed, because beans cooked in broth have a savoury creaminess that is akin to the best buttery mash. Combined with spicy Cajun kraut, jalapeño salsa and probiotic soured cream, this is a meal to feed both body and soul.

FOR THE VELVETY PINTO BEANS

200g (7oz) dried pinto beans

700ml (1¼ pints) chicken Bone Broth or Vegetable Broth (see pages 53–54)

3 garlic cloves, crushed

5 oregano sprigs

2 bay leaves

1 tablespoon chicken, bacon or duck fat, lard or olive oil

1 large onion, finely chopped

FOR THE JALAPEÑO SALSA

200g (7oz) sweet cherry tomatoes, roughly chopped

½ red onion, finely chopped

2 teaspoons sun-dried tomato paste

1 jalapeño chilli, de-seeded and finely chopped

Large handful of coriander leaves, roughly chopped

Juice of 1 lime

Sea salt

TO SERVE

8 soft corn tortillas

200g (7oz) soured cream

Cajun Kraut (see page 200) or other spicy pickle

2 limes, cut into wedges

For the pinto beans, soak the beans overnight in plenty of cold water. Drain and rinse the soaked beans and put them into a pan with the broth, garlic, oregano and bay leaves. Bring to the boil and boil rapidly for 5 minutes, then turn the heat right down, cover and let the beans simmer gently for about 1–1½ hours, until most of the broth is absorbed and the beans start to collapse. Discard the oregano stalks and bay leaves.

Melt the fat in a pan and sauté the onion gently until it is really sweet and soft, about 15 minutes. Add the pinto beans to the pan and mash them with a potato masher, leaving a little texture. Fry gently so that the bean mixture catches a little on the bottom of the pan, scraping up occasionally, until the beans have caramelised bits running through them, about 10 minutes. If the beans start to look a bit dry, add a little more broth or water until they look like creamy mash. Keep warm.

To make the salsa, combine the cherry tomatoes, red onion and sun-dried tomato paste in a serving bowl, then add chilli to your taste. Stir in the coriander and lime juice, adding salt to taste.

To serve, warm the tortillas, one at a time, in a dry frying pan over a high heat so that they catch a little, then remove and cover them with a slightly damp tea towel so they don't dry out.

Put the pinto beans, salsa, warm tortillas, soured cream, Cajun kraut and lime wedges on the table and let everyone help themselves. A crisp garden salad is a lovely accompaniment.

CRISPY LAMB WITH LEMONY FLAGEOLET BEANS AND ROAST TOMATOES

Serves 4

Slow-cooked lamb is a thing of beauty, but crisped up in a pan and scattered over soft, lemony beans, it becomes the sort of thing that people fight over. I always cook more than I need and stash some in the freezer for another day. Flageolet beans are relatively easy to digest for a pulse, so this would be a good entry-level dish if you are expanding your soluble fibre repertoire – start with a small portion if you're unsure.

200g (7oz) dried flageolet beans

2 teaspoons sea salt, plus extra for seasoning

6–7 large rosemary sprigs

1 lamb shoulder (about 2kg/4½lb)

400g (14oz) cherry vine tomatoes

Olive oil, for drizzling

2 garlic cloves, crushed

2 bay leaves

1 tablespoon chicken, bacon or duck fat or lard

1 large onion, finely chopped

50g (2oz) Preserved Lemons (see page 203), rind only, chopped

1 lemon, quartered

Put the dried beans in a large bowl, cover with plenty of cold water, stir in the salt, then leave the beans to soak overnight.

Preheat the oven to 160°C/140°C fan/gas 3. Put half of the rosemary sprigs into a roasting tray, place the lamb shoulder on top and cover with the remaining rosemary. Pour a little water into the tray, sprinkle the lamb with salt, cover with foil and roast for about 4 hours, until the meat is soft and tender. Remove the foil, turn the oven up to 200°C/180°C fan/gas 6 and roast for another 20–30 minutes, until the fat is crisp and golden.

Roast the tomatoes for the last hour of the lower oven temperature. To do this, put the tomatoes onto a baking sheet, drizzle with olive oil and sprinkle with salt. Roast until they are soft and starting to catch colour.

Meanwhile, drain the soaked flageolet beans, put them into a pan, cover with cold water, bring to the boil and boil rapidly for 5 minutes. Drain, rinse and return to the pan with the garlic and bay leaves. Cover with cold water, bring to the boil again and simmer gently until the beans are tender, about 40 minutes. Drain, reserving the beans and cooking water separately. Discard the bay leaves.

Melt the fat in an ovenproof pan and sauté the onion gently for about 20 minutes. Add the beans (and garlic if you like) and fry gently until the beans start to catch a little, about 10 minutes, then loosen with some of the reserved cooking water to make a creamy mixture. Off the heat, stir in the preserved lemon rind, then transfer it to the still warm oven.

Tear four small handfuls of lamb into bite-sized pieces. Put a heavy-based frying pan over a high heat and cook the lamb (without oil) until crispy on both sides, about 3–4 minutes per batch. Spoon the beans onto plates and spread it out a little, then top with crispy lamb shards and nestle the roast tomatoes and a lemon quarter alongside. Serve with steamed broccoli or greens.

FRAGRANT RICE WITH SPICED ROAST SQUASH AND BLACK BEANS

Serves 4

Short grain brown rice has a succulent quality and nutty flavour that make it a delicious partner for black beans. Slow cooking and roasting bring out the inherent sweetness in squash, tomatoes and red onions, and a generous hand with fragrant spices and punchy gremolata make this a meat-free meal that has incredible depth of flavour. It would also work with black rice and Camargue red rice.

200g (7oz) short grain brown rice

1 tablespoon olive oil

2 red onions, diced

3 celery sticks, diced

3 garlic cloves, finely chopped

1 tablespoon za'atar

1 tablespoon fennel seeds

2 tablespoons plus 1 teaspoon duck, chicken or bacon fat or coconut oil

1kg (2¼lb) squash (butternut, crown prince, harlequin, etc), peeled, de-seeded and cut into chip-sized wedges

2 teaspoons each cumin seeds, yellow mustard seeds and nigella seeds

350g (12oz) cherry vine tomatoes

250g (9oz) cooked black beans (125g/4½oz dried weight or 400g/14oz tin, rinsed and drained)

Finely grated zest of 1 lemon

600ml (1 pint) Bone Broth or Vegetable Broth (see pages 53–54) or water

50g (2oz) feta cheese, crumbled

Sea salt

FOR THE GREMOLATA

20g (¾oz) flat-leaf parsley, finely chopped

1 garlic clove, finely chopped

Finely grated zest of 1 lemon

Good pinch of sea salt

Lemon wedges, to serve

First, soak the rice in plenty of cold water for about 2 hours, then rinse and drain well.

Preheat the oven to 200°C/180°C fan/gas 6. Gently heat the olive oil in a large lidded frying pan (or casserole), add the red onions, celery, garlic, za'atar and fennel seeds and sauté gently for about 20 minutes, until the onions are soft, sweet and starting to colour.

Meanwhile, put 2 tablespoons of the fat into a roasting tray and place in the oven for a few minutes until melted. Toss the squash in it to coat and then sprinkle with some salt and the cumin, mustard and nigella seeds. Roast for about 45 minutes, until soft and a little charred on the edges.

Put the cherry tomatoes, still on their vines, onto another roasting tray greased with the remaining teaspoon of fat and roast these alongside the squash for the last 20 minutes, until the skins split and they smell sweet. Keep both the squash and tomatoes warm until the rice is ready.

Once the onions are softened, add the drained rice, the black beans, lemon zest and broth or water, season with a few good pinches of salt, then cover, bring to the boil and simmer for about 30–40 minutes, until the liquid is absorbed and the rice is soft and plump.

Put all the ingredients for the gremolata into a small bowl and stir to mix. Dish the rice into bowls and top with the roast tomatoes and a pile of roast squash. Scatter the gremolata and crumbled feta over the top and nestle a wedge of lemon in there too for people to squeeze onto their food.

CREAMY CHICKPEA POLENTA WITH MUSHROOMS AND CHICKEN LIVERS

Serves 4

Polenta made with chickpea flour is a soothing, creamy foil for the savoury mushrooms and chicken livers. Although polenta does require a little attention while it cooks, this chickpea version is rather more forgiving than maize. With such a diverse range of prebiotic fibre and little starch, this makes an incredibly satisfying meal that works equally well without the livers and with Parmesan in place of watercress.

4 tablespoons olive oil

1 onion, finely diced

160g (5½oz) chickpea (gram) flour

120g (4½oz) watercress, finely chopped

3 heaped tablespoons duck, chicken or goose fat

2 large red onions, halved and sliced

250g (9oz) chestnut mushrooms, sliced

12 sage leaves, finely chopped

300g (11oz) broccoli, cut into florets (you can use purple sprouting, but the stems can be chewy)

Handful of Almond Migas (see page 175) (optional)

400g (14oz) chicken livers

Oloroso or amontillado sherry, to taste

Sea salt and freshly ground black pepper

4 lemon wedges, to serve

Preheat the oven to 220°C/200°C fan/gas 7. Heat the olive oil in a largish pan, add the onion and sauté for about 10 minutes, until translucent.

Meanwhile, in a mixing bowl, gradually whisk 1 litre (1¾ pints) of cold water into the chickpea flour until it is all incorporated. Add the mixture to the onions and bring to the boil, whisking constantly, until it starts to thicken, then turn the heat down and continue to cook on the lowest heat for 25–30 minutes, stirring frequently. It should have the texture of a thick white sauce, so if it gets too thick, just add a little boiling water. When it tastes well cooked, season with salt and pepper and stir in the watercress. Keep warm. While the polenta cooks, heat a heaped tablespoon of the fat in a large saucepan or wok, add the red onions and fry over a medium heat until they start to catch some colour, about 10 minutes. Add the mushrooms and sage and fry for another few minutes, so that the mushrooms catch some colour, but do not become floppy. Scrape into a bowl and set aside briefly.

Put a heaped tablespoon of fat into a roasting tray and melt in the oven for a few minutes. Toss the broccoli in the fat until coated, season with salt and roast for 5–6 minutes, until the stalks are tender and a little charred on the edges. Scatter with almond migas if you have it.

Return the empty mushroom pan to a highish heat with the remaining fat and the chicken livers. Let the livers brown before turning them. When they are still pink inside and bronzed outside, add the mushroom mixture back to the pan, turn the heat up high and pour in a good splosh of sherry. Scrape any flavoursome bits off the bottom of the pan, check the livers are cooked (just pink but not bloody) and then tip everything into a bowl. Top each portion of polenta with the livers and a grind of black pepper. Nestle the broccoli alongside and serve with a fresh lemon wedge.

SAGE AND ONION QUICHE WITH A CHESTNUT CRUST

Serves 4

Melting, sweet chestnut flour and fava bean flour combine beautifully to make a thin, crisp crust for this creamy quiche. Using yoghurt in the pastry and resting for longer helps to make the fava bean flour more digestible, while still providing your microbes with a fantastic supper. If you don't have chestnut flour, oat or rye flour would work too.

FOR THE CHESTNUT CRUST
80g (3oz) chestnut flour
120g (4oz) fava bean flour (or chickpea or yellow pea flour)
40g (1½oz) ground linseed
2 pinches of sea salt
120g (4oz) cold salted butter, diced
160g (5oz) live Greek-style yoghurt

FOR THE SAGE AND ONION FILLING
25g (1oz) salted butter
3 large onions, halved and thickly sliced
10–15 sage leaves, finely chopped
2 large pinches of sea salt
225ml (8fl oz) double cream
3 large organic eggs
25g (1oz) finely grated Parmesan

Make the chestnut crust. Put the chestnut and fava bean flours, ground linseed and salt into a mixing bowl and mix briefly. Rub in the butter with your fingertips until it resembles coarse breadcrumbs, then use a butter knife to stir in half of the yoghurt. Add the remaining yoghurt gradually, until the mixture starts to clump together, then gather it into a ball and knead gently on the worktop into a smooth pastry. Form into a disc, wrap in baking parchment and chill in the fridge for at least 12 hours and up to 48 hours.

For the filling, melt the butter in a large pan, add the onions, sage and salt and sauté gently for about 30 minutes, until the onions have reduced by half their volume and are golden and sweet.

While the onions cook, roll out the pastry case. line the base of a 23cm (9in) loose-based tart tin with a circle of baking parchment. Knead the pastry for a minute to soften it up. Lay a piece of clingfilm on the worktop, place the chilled pastry on top and lay a sheet of clingfilm over the pastry. Roll the pastry into a circle large enough to line the tart tin, peel off the top layer of clingfilm and invert over the tart tin. Ease the pastry into the corners before you remove the clingfilm and trim the top edge with a sharp knife. Keep the scraps in case you need to patch the crust.

Preheat the oven to 180°C/160°C fan/gas 4. Line the tart case with baking parchment, fill with baking beans and bake for 10 minutes, then remove the parchment and beans and bake for another 5 minutes. If there are any cracks, soften a bit of the remaining pastry with water and use it as putty to fill them.

Scrape the softened onions into the pastry case and level, then whisk the cream, eggs and Parmesan together and pour evenly over the onions. Bake for 25–30 minutes, until the filling is pale gold, a little risen and just set.

Serve with a pile of delicious salad leaves and Green Potato Salad (see page 157).

BAKED COD WITH A PISTACHIO CRUST

Serves 4

Pistachio nuts have a delicate creaminess that works well with mild-flavoured fish and are full of the fibre that your gut loves. Sourdough crumbs add welcome savouriness; I use gluten-free sourdough made from teff or buckwheat, but rye or spelt would be delicious, too. You can freeze the raw crumb mixture and use frozen fish to make this a super quick workday supper.

120g (4½oz) shelled pistachio nuts, finely chopped

90g (3¼oz) sourdough breadcrumbs

30g (1¼oz) flat-leaf parsley leaves (2 large handfuls), finely chopped

1 teaspoon flaked sea salt

Few good grinds of black pepper

700g (1lb 9oz) sustainable cod fillet (or hake, pollock or similar)

200g (7oz) live natural yoghurt

Preheat the oven to 220°C/200°C fan/gas 7. Line a baking sheet with baking parchment. Put the pistachios, breadcrumbs, parsley, salt and black pepper into a mixing bowl and mix well, then set aside.

Remove the skin from the fish and slice the fillet into four portions. Put the yoghurt onto a dinner plate or into a wide, shallow bowl, and put the pistachio mixture onto another dinner plate, both wide enough to make coating the fish easy.

Take a portion of fish and place it in the yoghurt, turning to coat completely, then place in the pistachio mixture and spoon the crumbs over the top to coat all over. Transfer to the lined baking sheet and repeat with the remaining fish portions.

Bake for 12–15 minutes, according to the thickness of your portions, until the fish is just opaque and flakes when tested with a fork.

Serve with a chicory salad and Griddled Courgettes (see page 64), or creamy Parsnip Mash (see page 78) and buttered, steamed greens.

SOOTHING DAL WITH PLUM CHUTNEY
AND ROAST RADISHES

Serves 4

Dal is a delicately spiced sauce made from split peas or lentils that can be either porridgy or thin as a soup, according to your whim. Split mung beans (moong dal) make the most easily digested dal, so if you're adding pulses to your diet, this is a great intro dish. Although this might seem like lots of work, preparation is simple and everything keeps well, so it's excellent to stash in the fridge for a couple of days for a weekday supper, then reheat (remember to cool and chill the cooked rice quickly, or cool and freeze it flat in freezer bags, then reheat from frozen). When plums are not available, try mango or even eating apples.

FOR THE SOOTHING DAL

200g (7oz) moong dal (or other split peas or split lentils)

2 tablespoons ghee (or duck or chicken fat)

1 large onion, finely chopped

1 tablespoon coriander seeds

25g (1oz) fresh turmeric root, peeled and finely grated (or 1 teaspoon ground turmeric)

2–3 garlic cloves, finely chopped

1 teaspoon grated fresh root ginger

1–2 teaspoons chilli powder

1 tablespoon tomato purée

750ml (24fl oz) boiling water

1 teaspoon sea salt

2 tablespoons yellow mustard seeds

1 teaspoon cumin seeds

Juice of ½ lemon

Small bunch of coriander leaves

FOR THE COCONUT RICE

350g (12oz) brown basmati rice

400ml (14fl oz) boiling water

400ml (14fl oz) tin coconut milk

10 green cardamom pods, cracked open

Pinch of sea salt

For the soothing dal, rinse the moong dal and soak for about 2 hours in plenty of cold water, then drain and rinse well. Soak the basmati rice for the coconut rice at the same time in a separate bowl.

Melt 1 tablespoon of the ghee in a pan, then sauté the onion gently for about 5 minutes, while you prepare the aromatics. Grind the coriander seeds using a pestle and mortar, then add to the onion with the turmeric, garlic, ginger and a teaspoon of the chilli powder. Cook gently for about 25 minutes, until the onion is sweet and soft. Stir in the tomato purée and cook a few minutes more, then add the drained moong dal and the boiling water. Bring to a simmer, then cover and cook for about an hour, until the moong dal has the consistency of a thick soup. Add the salt and more chilli powder if you like and then use a balloon whisk to beat the dal to a velvety smoothness.

About 40 minutes before the dal is ready, finish the coconut rice. Drain the rice and rinse well, then put into a lidded pan with the boiling water, coconut milk, cardamom pods and salt. Bring to the boil, then reduce to a simmer, cover and cook undisturbed until the liquid is all absorbed, about 30 minutes (check by parting the grains to see the bottom of the pan). Turn off the heat, but leave covered for 10 minutes, then fluff up with a fork (pick out the cardamom pods before serving).

FOR THE ROAST RADISHES

600g (1lb 5oz) small pink radishes, trimmed (leave a little tuft of green leaves on, if they have them – the weight given is without leaves)

Olive oil, for drizzling

4–5 bay leaves

20g (¾oz) nigella seeds

Few pinches of sea salt

FOR THE PLUM CHUTNEY

400g (14oz) greengages or sweet plums, stoned and quartered

1½ teaspoons cider vinegar

1 teaspoon grated fresh root ginger

Meanwhile, put the radishes on to roast while the rice cooks. Preheat the oven to 180°C/160°C fan/gas 4. Put the radishes on a baking tray, drizzle generously with olive oil and then shake the tray so the radishes are evenly coated. Tuck the bay leaves underneath and scatter with the nigella seeds and salt. Roast for about 30 minutes, until they are just soft to a toothpick. Discard the bay leaves before serving.

In the meantime, to make the plum chutney, put the greengages or plums into a small pan with the vinegar, ginger and 125ml (4fl oz) of water. Cover and cook until the fruit collapses, about 10 minutes.

To finish the dal, heat the remaining ghee in a frying pan and gently fry the mustard and cumin seeds until they start to pop, about 2–3 minutes, then stir them into the dal with the lemon juice. Stir in the coriander leaves, or scatter them over the dish.

Put everything into pretty bowls and let people help themselves. Some thick live natural yoghurt and steamed greens are a good accompaniment.

TREATS

PANELLE

A VERY DECADENT CHOCOLATE AND CHERRY TORTE

FIG AND PUMPKIN SEED CRACKERS WITH RAW CHEESE AND FIG BUTTER

ROAST PLUMS WITH VANILLA YOGHURT AND PEANUT BUTTER CRUMBLE

FIG AND ORANGE CHOCOLATE BABYCAKES

Join me in a decadent romp through the chocolatiest torte you ever did taste
(that just happens to contain beans); peanut butter crumble that tastes of cookies,
but delights your microbes; crisp hot panelle dipped into probiotic ketchup as soon as
they are cool enough to touch; and finish with a raw cheese board and some moreishly
figgy crackers. Everything here is prebiotic, but don't worry, it doesn't taste 'good for you',
it really does taste good.

PANELLE

Serves 4 as part of a meal

Panelle are a traditional Sicilian treat made from a chickpea polenta formed into little pancakes on the back of a plate and then fried. I simply pour mine into a container and cut into chips when cold, then deep-fry until they are deep gold and crisp outside but soft inside. Nothing deep-fried is ever a health food, but the chickpeas will delight your microbes and they make a fantastic alternative to chips.

115g (4¼oz) chickpea flour

2 tablespoons Sourdough Starter (see pages 35–37) (optional)

2 tablespoons olive oil, plus extra for greasing

2 pinches of fine sea salt, plus extra to serve

500g (1lb 2oz) lard or beef dripping

Probiotic Ketchup (see page 228), to serve

Put the chickpea flour, sourdough starter (if using) and 250ml (9fl oz) of water in a mixing bowl and beat together using a whisk, until smooth. Cover and set aside at room temperature for 3–24 hours (but if you choose the longer time, it should go in the fridge after 3 hours). You don't need to add sourdough starter, but it will make the panelle easier to digest, or you could use live natural yoghurt as an alternative.

Oil the inside of a 20cm (8in) square heatproof container or deep-sided tray/baking tin and set aside. When the time is up, whisk the olive oil and salt into the chickpea mixture until incorporated, then pour into a pan. Set the pan over a high heat and whisk the chickpea mixture constantly, scraping the bottom of the pan, for about 20 minutes until the mixture is a very thick polenta consistency. Pour into the prepared container or tray/tin, leave to cool for about 30 minutes, then chill in the fridge for a few hours until completely set (overnight is ideal).

When you are ready to fry the panelle, set a high-sided, heavy-based pan over a highish heat and melt your fat; when a cube of bread browns in under a minute it is hot enough, but if it's smoking, it's too hot! Tip the panelle mixture out onto a chopping board, pat dry with kitchen paper and cut into chip shapes. Deep-fry the panelle in batches (don't overcrowd the pan, otherwise the fat will cool) for 4–5 minutes per batch, until deep gold. Drain on kitchen paper, sprinkle with a little fine salt and be careful not to burn your mouth. It is best to eat the panelle as soon as possible before they lose their crispness. Serve with the ketchup.

A VERY DECADENT CHOCOLATE AND CHERRY TORTE

Serves 8

This deeply chocolatey torte has a fudgy, light yet dense texture that will have chocolate lovers offering to give you their firstborn for another slice. As with all sweet things, eat this joyfully, but only occasionally, and with a little glint in your eye as you wait to tell your guests that their luscious dessert contained beans.

140g (5oz) salted butter, plus extra for greasing

200g (7oz) dark chocolate (70 per cent cocoa solids), roughly chopped

2 large organic eggs

175g (6oz) dark muscovado sugar

2 teaspoons vanilla extract

1 teaspoon baking powder

150g (5oz) cold cooked adzuki beans (about 70g dried beans)

45g (1½oz) brown teff flour (or rye or chestnut flour)

225ml (8fl oz) double cream

3–4 teaspoons Cherry Heering liqueur (or vanilla extract and a drizzle of raw honey) (optional)

300g (11oz) fresh cherries, with stalks attached

Preheat the oven to 190°C/170°C fan/gas 5. Butter and line the base and sides of a 23cm (9in) round springform cake tin with baking parchment. Melt the butter and chocolate in a heatproof bowl over a pan of barely simmering water, stir to combine, then set aside to cool a little.

Put the eggs, sugar, vanilla extract, baking powder and cooked beans into a blender and whizz until the mixture is completely smooth. Scrape into a mixing bowl. Using a balloon whisk, beat the melted chocolate mixture into the bean mixture in four even additions, beating well between each addition, until the mixture becomes glossy again. Sift the flour into the bowl and fold in gently just until combined.

Pour into the prepared cake tin and bake for about 20 minutes, until the top has set but there is still some wobble left. A cake tester inserted will bring out some gooey crumbs. Cool completely in the tin and then unmould onto a serving plate.

Just before serving, softly whip the cream and ripple the cherry liqueur (if using) through it before piling it up in the centre of the torte. Top with the cherries. Once dressed, eat straight away or store in the fridge and eat within 24 hours. Undressed, the torte will last a few days stored in an airtight container.

FIG AND PUMPKIN SEED CRACKERS WITH RAW CHEESE AND FIG BUTTER

Makes about 30

Figs lend these crackers a subtle sweetness and chew, with those wonderful seeds that pop under your teeth. High in both soluble and insoluble fibre, omega fats and resistant starch, they make a deeply satisfying end to a meal when paired with some delicious unpasteurised cheese and moreish fig butter. Try making them with brazil nuts and black raisins in place of the fig and pumpkin seeds, for a very grown-up garibaldi cracker.

50g (2oz) whole golden linseeds

20g (¾oz) salted butter

100ml (3½fl oz) boiling water

200g (7oz) dried figs, finely chopped (so they have the texture of mincemeat)

120g (4½oz) pumpkin seeds, finely chopped or coarsely ground

50g (2oz) ground golden linseed

70g (2½oz) white teff or rye flour, plus extra for dusting

4 pinches of sea salt, plus extra to sprinkle

½ teaspoon freshly ground black pepper, plus extra to sprinkle

Unpasteurised* cheese and Fermented Fig Butter (see page 204), to serve

*Please check medical recommendations for cheeses to avoid if pregnant, immunodeficient or for children under three.

Preheat the oven to 150°C/130°C fan/gas 2 and have ready three baking sheets. Put the whole linseeds and butter into a small heatproof bowl and pour over the boiling water. Leave for 10 minutes to allow the linseeds to soak up the water and form a gel.

Put the figs, pumpkin seeds, ground linseed, teff or rye flour, salt and black pepper into a mixing bowl and scrape in the soaked linseeds. Use your hands to knead into a firm dough. If the dough feels too sticky, just put a little flour on the work surface and knead in for a minute or so. Divide the dough into three equal pieces.

To roll out the crackers, tear off three pieces of baking parchment, each the size of a baking sheet, or use flexible silicone baking mats. Sprinkle a little flour over one sheet of parchment, place one portion of the dough on top and cover with a sheet of clingfilm. Roll out to the depth of the seeds, as thin as it will go. Lift the clingfilm, sprinkle the dough with a little extra salt and pepper, then replace the clingfilm and gently roll the seasoning into the dough. Mark the dough into long, thin crackers with a pizza cutter or press down with a sharp knife (don't drag it through the dough) to make the marks. Transfer the marked dough (still on the parchment paper) onto a baking sheet. Repeat with the remaining dough.

Bake for about 25–30 minutes, until golden and crisp – if there is any flex in the centre when you press, put them back in the oven again. Cool on the baking sheets for 10 minutes, then transfer to a wire rack and leave to cool completely, before breaking into crackers to serve. Serve with unpasteurised cheese and fermented fig butter. These crackers will keep in an airtight box for up to 10 days.

ROAST PLUMS WITH VANILLA YOGHURT AND PEANUT BUTTER CRUMBLE

Serves 4

Stone fruit that is a little firm becomes tender and sweet from the heat of the oven. In this recipe, the crumble is kept separate, so it stays crisp against the juicy fruit and creamy yoghurt. I warn you now that if you're a fan of peanut butter cookies you won't be able to resist any leftovers, so you may need to hide them for your own good. Plums, peanuts, linseed and teff (or rye) contain lots of soluble fibre for the friendly bacteria in the yoghurt to munch on.

FOR THE PEANUT BUTTER CRUMBLE

90g (3¼oz) brown teff, buckwheat, chestnut or rye flour

60g (2¼oz) ground linseed

80g (3oz) light muscovado sugar

3 good pinches of sea salt

50g (2oz) chilled salted butter, diced

130g (4½oz) unsweetened peanut butter (or Sunflower Seed Butter, see page 124)

2 teaspoons vanilla extract

FOR THE ROAST PLUMS

16 plums or greengages, halved and stoned

20–60g (¾–2¼oz) light muscovado sugar

FOR THE VANILLA YOGHURT

400g (14oz) live Greek-style yoghurt

1 tablespoon light muscovado sugar

Seeds from ½ vanilla pod or 1 teaspoon vanilla extract

Preheat the oven to 180°C/160°C fan/gas 4. Line a baking sheet with parchment paper. First, make the peanut butter crumble. Put the flour, ground linseed, sugar and salt in a bowl and rub in the butter until the mixture looks like breadcrumbs. Add the peanut butter and cut it through the mixture with a butter knife, until it is well mixed, then sprinkle the vanilla extract over and mix this in. The mixture should start to form clumps at this stage, but if it still looks quite dry, add a couple of teaspoons of cold water and turn it over with your fingers until it starts to form clumps.

Tip onto the lined baking sheet and spread out roughly, then bake for 15–18 minutes, until the crumble mix feels firm when you press it gently. Cool completely on the baking sheet – it will crisp up on cooling. Leave the oven on and turn the temperature up to 200°C/180°C fan/gas 6, so while the crumble is cooling, roast the plums.

Put the plums or greengages, cut side up, into a roasting tray, placing them close together. Sprinkle with 20g (¾oz) of the sugar if they are reasonably sweet or 40g (1½oz) or more if they are tart. Roast for 20–30 minutes, until they are soft and the juices have run. Set aside to cool slightly (the plums can be served warm or cool).

For the vanilla yoghurt, put the yoghurt and sugar into a mixing bowl with the vanilla seeds or extract and stir well to combine.

Put the crumble, plums and yoghurt on the table and let everyone help themselves – the tray of plums looks lovely this way.

FIG AND ORANGE CHOCOLATE BABYCAKES

Serves 4

Although these rich, melting morsels of chocolate sponge do contain some very beneficial ingredients, their main purpose is to bring you joy. There is at least one study to show that the more you enjoy your food, the more nutrients you absorb. So treat yourself to these babycakes every so often, safe in the knowledge that each gooey spoonful is delighting your microbes almost as much as your taste buds.

90g (3¼oz) dried figs (or stoned prunes), chopped into small pieces

120g (4½oz) salted butter, diced, plus extra for greasing

120g (4½oz) dark chocolate (70 per cent cocoa solids), roughly chopped

2 large organic eggs, separated

2 large organic egg yolks

20g (¾oz) brown teff flour (or rye or chestnut flour), plus extra for dusting

Finely grated zest of 1 large orange

Pinch of sea salt

120g (4½oz) dark muscovado sugar

4 dariole moulds or small teacups

Generously butter the dariole moulds or teacups, dust with flour and then chill in the fridge. Put the figs into a small pan with 100ml (3½fl oz) of water, cover and bring to the boil, then simmer until all the water is absorbed, about 10–15 minutes. Leave to cool completely.

Preheat the oven to 220°C/200°C fan/gas 7. Melt the butter and chocolate in a heatproof bowl over a pan of barely simmering water, stir to combine, then set aside to cool a little. Stir all the egg yolks, the flour, orange zest and soaked figs into the cooled chocolate mixture until incorporated, then set aside.

Whisk the egg whites with the salt in a clean mixing bowl using an electric whisk, until frothy and opaque, then tip in the sugar and whisk again until it forms a stiff, shiny meringue. It won't hold stiff peaks, but it will hold its shape well. Gently fold the meringue into the chocolate mixture, just until there is no white showing.

Scrape the mixture into the prepared moulds or teacups, dividing evenly, then bake for about 8 minutes, until risen and firm on the top, but still wobbly if pressed. The top should look like cake, not glossy at all. If you don't want a gooey centre, bake the cakes for 10-12 minutes in total.

Leave for a couple of minutes to settle – the centres will fall. Check that the cakes are not stuck around the edge and then tip each one out onto a plate and tuck in! Softly whipped cream makes an excellent companion.

HEAL

PICKLED & PRESERVED

KIMCHI

CAJUN KRAUT

PICKLED BABY COURGETTES

SUNSHINE SAUERKRAUT

PRESERVED LEMONS

FERMENTED FIG BUTTER

SWEET SPRING ONIONS

RADISH AND POMEGRANATE PICKLES

RADISH BOMBS

RIBBON PICKLE

LABNEH

PRESERVED LABNEH

This chapter is a gentle introduction to the wonders of lacto fermenting. If you have never fermented anything before, you might imagine exploding jars of noxious mixtures, but pickling is simply a case of mixing the right amount of salt with some vegetables and allowing the friendly bacteria to flourish and transform your mixture into a sweet and sour delight.

Pickles are probiotic because of the friendly bacteria they contain and are a great thing to add to all sorts of meals to give them a little piquant kick. Once you get the hang of the methods in this chapter, you can start to experiment with different vegetables and make your own pickled creations. Fermenting works best at slightly cooler temperatures than in many modern houses, so find a cooler spot out of direct sunlight. If you are unsure about how to tell whether your pickles are ready, invest in some PH indicator strips and bring out your budding scientist (ranges are given in the recipes). It's as simple as dipping the strip into the pickle and checking the colour on a chart.

KIMCHI

Makes 1 litre (1¾ pints)

Kimchi is a type of sauerkraut from Korea that is fiery, garlicky, gingery and piquant. Usually made with napa or Chinese cabbage, which is a little drier than European cabbage, it is brined first to soften it before all the delicious aromatics are added. Make this as punchy as you like and add it to stir fries, salads, rice and anything else that needs a fragrant chilli hit – just add it after cooking to preserve the friendly bacteria.

1 large Chinese cabbage or pointed cabbage, quartered

65g (2¼oz) sea salt

1.5 litres (2½ pints) filtered or mineral water

2 large carrots, grated

Bunch of spring onions, washed and roughly chopped

3–5 fat garlic cloves, finely chopped

½–1 teaspoon chilli powder

1 tablespoon grated fresh root ginger

1 tablespoon sweet paprika

½–1 tablespoon dried chilli flakes

½–1 tablespoon fish sauce (nam pla) (optional)

2-litre (3½-pint) preserving jar
Smaller jars, for storage

The night before you plan to make your kimchi, brine your cabbage. Put the cabbage into a non-reactive bowl. Add the salt to the water, stirring until dissolved, then pour this over the cabbage and leave to soak for about 8–12 hours.

Reserve 500ml of the cabbage brine. Drain and roughly chop the brined cabbage and put into a large mixing bowl with all the remaining ingredients, but only add half of the chilli flakes. Using clean hands, mix well and massage until the cabbage starts to look a little softer and the juices start to flow, about 2–3 minutes. Taste and add more chilli flakes or fish sauce, if you like.

Wash your preserving jar with hot, soapy water (no need to sterilise), rinse well and then pile everything into it. Press down really firmly with clean fingers or a rolling pin until the juices come up to the top of the vegetables. To hold the vegetables under the liquid, place a ziplock freezer bag into the jar and pour enough brine into the bag so that the juices come up around it. Zip up the bag, cover with a clean tea towel and leave to ferment at cool room temperature (19–20°C) for 10–14 days.

Your kimchi is ready when it tastes pleasantly sour, but is not fizzy on the tongue (a PH indicator strip will read between 3.2 and 4). Taste it after 10 days using a clean fork, but you can allow up to 14 days for it to become properly sour. When it is ready, transfer to clean smaller jars, squash it down well, seal and keep it in the fridge where it will keep for up to 9 months. Open and reseal the jars once daily for the first few days of refrigeration to release any gas.

Clockwise from top left:
Radish Bombs (see page 208), Sweet Spring Onions (see page 206), Ribbon Pickle (see page 209), Preserved Lemons (see page 203), Kimchi (see above) and Pickled Baby Courgettes (see page 201).

CAJUN KRAUT

Makes 1 litre (1¾ pints)

Sauerkraut gets a little taste of Louisiana with some Cajun spices that make it a perfect partner for meals like Burritos (see page 163), Tacos (see page 170) or any slow-cooked or barbecued meat. The heat comes from chilli, mustard and black pepper, so add the spices slowly until the kraut tastes as spicy as you like it. It's also fantastic with some strong cheese, making an especially probiotic treat if the cheese is made with raw milk.

1 large white cabbage or spring cabbage, finely sliced (woody parts discarded)

2 large carrots, peeled and shaved into long strips (using the peeler)

½ bunch of spring onions, white and pale green parts only, sliced, or 1 red or white onion, finely chopped

1 eating apple, cored and finely diced

2–3 fat garlic cloves, finely chopped

About 20g (¾oz) sea salt (see method)

½–1 teaspoon chilli powder

1 tablespoon paprika

1 teaspoon fennel seeds

1 teaspoon cumin seeds

1 teaspoon mustard powder or Dijon mustard without preservatives

Few good grinds of black pepper

2-litre (3½-pint) preserving jar
½ quantity of brine (see page 198)
Smaller jars, for storage

Weigh the prepared vegetables, apple and garlic so you can work out the salt needed. When you have your weight, you need to add 2 per cent salt to the mixture, so for 1kg (2¼lb) vegetables, you'll add 20g (¾oz) of salt (it doesn't matter if you're a little out). Weigh out the salt and set aside.

Put the prepared vegetables, apple, garlic and all the remaining ingredients except the salt (and only half of the chilli powder) into a large mixing bowl and then add half of the measured salt. Using clean hands, mix well and massage until the cabbage starts to look a little softer and the juices start to flow, about 2–3 minutes. Taste and add more of the salt, mixing and massaging a bit more, until the mixture tastes salty, but not unpalatably so. Add the remaining chilli powder, if you like.

Wash your preserving jar with hot, soapy water (no need to sterilise), rinse well and then pile everything into it. Press down really firmly with clean fingers or a rolling pin until the juices come up to the top of the vegetables. To hold the vegetables under the liquid, place a ziplock freezer bag into the jar and pour enough brine into the bag so that the juices come up around it. Zip up the bag, cover with a clean tea towel and leave to ferment at cool room temperature (19–20°C) for 7–10 days.

Your kraut is ready when it tastes pleasantly sour but is not fizzy on the tongue (a PH indicator strip will read between 3.2 and 4). Taste it after 7 days using a clean fork, but you can allow up to 10 days for it to become properly sour. When it is ready, transfer to clean smaller jars, squash it down well, then close up the jars and store in the fridge where it will keep for up to 9 months. Open and reseal the jars once daily for the first few days of refrigeration to release any gas.

PICKLED BABY COURGETTES

Makes 750g–1kg (1lb 10oz–2¼lb)

Pickled courgettes are a little like gherkins, but fermenting your own gherkins can be fraught
with disappointment as cucumbers contain an enzyme that can make them mushy. Not so with
courgettes. If you grow your own this is a wonderful way to preserve the babies for autumn,
when you will have recovered your fondness for courgettes but have none in the garden.

30g (1¼oz) fine sea salt

10g (¼oz) caster sugar

1 litre (1¾ pints) filtered or mineral water

750g–1kg (1lb 10oz–2¼lb) baby courgettes, stalk ends trimmed

1–3 garlic cloves, halved

2 basil sprigs or a head of dill flowers

Blackcurrant leaves or vine leaves, rinsed (optional)

2-litre (3½-pint) preserving jar

Smaller jars, for storage

Wash your preserving jar with hot, soapy water (no need to sterilise) and
rinse well. Make the brine by stirring the salt and sugar into the water until
dissolved. Stand the courgettes on their ends in the preserving jar and pack
in as many as you can. If you need to, any remaining courgettes can lie on
top of these. Tuck the garlic in around the courgettes and poke the basil or
dill down the side of the jar.

Tuck the blackcurrant or vine leaves over the courgettes if you are using
them – these provide a little tannin that keeps your pickles crisper. Pour
the brine in to cover by at least 2.5cm (1in). You will need a weight to keep
everything down, so open a ziplock freezer bag, place it into the jar and fill
it with any spare brine.

Cover the jar with a clean tea towel and leave to ferment at cool room
temperature (19–20°C) for 5–6 days. After 3–4 days, the courgettes will
start to look a little duller in colour. Taste them after 5 days to see if
they are sour enough (a PH indicator strip will read between 3.2 and 4).
When they are ready, remove the leaves, herbs and garlic and transfer the
courgettes to clean smaller jars. Top with fresh leaves (if you have them, as
these will help to keep the courgettes firm) and ensure the courgettes are
always submerged in the brine. These pickles will keep in the fridge for up
to 6 months.

SUNSHINE SAUERKRAUT

Makes 1.25 litres (2¼ pints)

This delicious sauerkraut has a gorgeous yellow colour and delicate floral flavour, unique to anti-inflammatory turmeric. Black pepper really brings out the subtle nutty and aniseed flavours of the vegetables and provides lovely background warmth. Salsify and celeriac contain lots of gut-friendly inulin, making this a fantastic prebiotic addition to meals.

2 salsify or scorzonera roots (or parsnips), washed, peeled and thinly sliced

Finely grated zest of 1 lemon, plus juice of ½ lemon

½ celeriac, peeled and sliced into thin matchsticks

1 large white cabbage or pointed cabbage

½ bunch of spring onions, white and pale green parts only, sliced, or 1 small onion, finely chopped

1 garlic clove, finely chopped

2 tablespoons finely grated fresh turmeric root (use gloves to prepare this!)

½ teaspoon freshly ground black pepper

About 20g (¾oz) sea salt (see method)

2-litre (3½-pint) preserving jar
½ quantity of brine (see page 198)
Smaller jars, for storage

Put the salsify into a large mixing bowl with the lemon zest and juice and toss to coat in the juice to prevent it oxidising. Add the celeriac, turning to coat well in the lemon juice. Save a couple of the outer leaves of the cabbage, then finely slice the remainder, discarding the really woody parts.

Add the cabbage, onions, garlic, turmeric and black pepper to the salsify and celeriac and mix. Weigh the ingredients at this point so you can work out the salt needed. When you have your weight, you need to add 2 per cent salt to the mixture, so for 1kg (2¼lb) vegetables, you'll add 20g (¾oz) of salt. Weigh out the salt.

Add half of the measured salt to the vegetable mixture and massage a little using clean hands (I wear clean gloves to avoid staining mine). Taste for saltiness and add more of the salt, mixing and massaging a bit more, until the vegetables taste salty, but not unpalatably so. The mixture should taste subtle and yummy.

Wash your preserving jar with hot, soapy water (no need to sterilise), rinse well and then pile everything into it. Press down really firmly with clean fingers or a rolling pin until the juices come up to the top of the vegetables. Place the reserved cabbage leaves on top of the sauerkraut. To hold the vegetables under the liquid, place a ziplock freezer bag into the jar and pour enough brine into the bag so that the juices come up around it. Zip up the bag, cover with a clean tea towel and leave to ferment at cool room temperature (19–20°C) for 7–14 days.

Your sauerkraut is ready when it tastes pleasantly sour but is not fizzy on the tongue. Taste it after 7 days using a clean fork, but you can allow up to 14 days for it to become properly sour (a PH indicator strip will read between 3.2 and 4). When it is ready, transfer to clean smaller jars, squash it down well, close up the jars and keep in the fridge where it will keep for several months. Open and reseal the jars once daily for the first few days of refrigeration to release any gas.

PRESERVED LEMONS

Makes 8 preserved lemons

Salty, fragrant preserved lemons are a delicious addition to rich meat dishes, summer salads, roast chicken or even vanilla ice cream. Once you get the taste for them you might find yourself sneaking them into any number of meals! As they are so salty, don't add salt to dishes until after you have added the preserved lemon. Traditionally, only the skin is used, but you can decide for yourself whether to discard the pulp.

8 organic lemons, washed in cool water and dried

150g (5oz) sea salt

Juice of about 4–6 extra lemons

Olive oil

1.5-litre (2½-pint) preserving jar

½ quantity of brine (see page 198)

Smaller jars, for storage

Wash the preserving jar with hot, soapy water (no need to sterilise) and rinse well. Cut about 1cm (½in) off the stalk end of a lemon and cut it in half lengthways, almost all the way to the bottom, but stop short, so the lemon is still intact at the bottom. Repeat this cut so the lemon is quartered but remains intact at the bottom.

Over a bowl, take a tablespoon of the salt and squash this evenly into the cavity now formed by opening out the lemon like a flower. Squeeze the lemon back together and wedge into the jar. Repeat the cutting and salting with the remaining lemons, squashing each one firmly into place in the jar as you go.

When all the lemons are salted, use the end of a clean rolling pin or your fist to squash the lemons down into the preserving jar as much as possible without making the lemons disintegrate. Juices should start to come out of the lemons to about halfway up. Tip in any remaining salt and top up with lemon juice until the lemons are covered and will remain under the lemon brine when you squash them down a little.

Press a ziplock freezer bag over the lemons and fill with enough brine to weight the lemons down and form an airlock. Close up the jar, without the rubber seal, or use an airlock (see page 22). Leave the lemons to ferment at cool room temperature (19–20°C) for at least 6 weeks and then check them to see that the skin is soft. If not, leave for up to 10 weeks.

When they are ready, transfer to clean smaller jars and cover with the lemon brine, then pour about 1cm (½in) olive oil on top of the brine to prevent oxidisation, close up the jars and refrigerate for up to 6 months. Alternatively, drain off all the brine, pack the lemons into clean smaller jars, top up with olive oil until completely covered, then close up the jars. They will keep in the larder like this for 6–9 months. Use a clean fork to get the lemons out of the jar.

FERMENTED FIG BUTTER

Makes about 600g (1lb 5oz)

Fig butter has nothing to do with butter, but everything to do with figs! Essentially it's a kind of jam and pie filling hybrid made from dried figs and aromatics, fermented using the whey that drains out when you make labneh. This is a prebiotic, probiotic treat that you will find yourself sneaking a spoonful of when nobody is looking. I first saw a recipe for this in Sandor Ellix Katz's book *The Art of Fermentation* and fashioned myself something a little simpler with classic Spanish flavours of anise and orange. It's a little bit like Christmas in a jar.

600g (1lb 5oz) dried figs, roughly chopped

600ml (1 pint) tepid water

Finely grated zest of 2 oranges

1 teaspoon fine sea salt

4 tablespoons fresh whey from Labneh (see page 210)

½ teaspoon anise seeds

1-litre (1¾-pint) preserving jar

½ quantity of brine (see page 198)

Wash your preserving jar with hot, soapy water (no need to sterilise) and rinse well. Put the figs into a bowl, cover with the tepid water and leave to soak for 15 minutes, then drain and reserve the figs and water separately.

Put the soaked figs into a food-processor with all the remaining ingredients and process until it is the texture of very thick apple purée or chop finely by hand. If you need to loosen it, add a little of the reserved soaking water.

Scrape the mixture into your preserving jar, smooth down the surface and press a piece of baking parchment onto the top. Follow with a ziplock freezer bag and fill this with enough brine so that it will form a weight (you can also use clean coins, pebbles or baking beans in the bag). Zip up the bag, remove the rubber seal if the jar has one and close up the jar loosely to allow any gases to escape (there won't be much).

Leave to ferment at room temperature (20–22°C) for 36–48 hours. You can let it start to bubble, but I tend to put it in the fridge when it has just taken on the merest hint of sourness. The risk with fermenting fruit is that alcohol can start to form if you let it go too long, so err on the side of caution.

Take out the weight, replace the rubber seal, close up the jar and move to the fridge to slowly ferment for another month. Release any gas by opening the lid daily for the first week of refrigeration. After a month it is ready to eat and will keep for up to 6 months in the fridge. Replace the baking parchment each time you use it.

SWEET SPRING ONIONS

Makes 300g (11oz)

These mild, sweet pickled onions are a great probiotic addition to a rich meal, cutting through heavy food and aiding digestion. It is a two-step process with vinegar and honey added partway through the ferment.

500g (1lb 2oz) spring onions, trimmed (or peeled shallots, halved if large)

20g (¾oz) sea salt

1 litre (1¾ pints) filtered or mineral water

1 tablespoon runny raw honey

2 tablespoons cider vinegar or rice vinegar

1-litre (1¾-pint) preserving jar without rubber seal

1 piece of yoghurt pot plastic to use as a follower or similar

Wash your preserving jar with hot, soapy water (no need to sterilise) and rinse well. Cut off the darker green parts of the spring onions – you will just use the white and light green parts for this pickle as the darker parts go mushy. Make the brine by stirring the salt into the water until dissolved.

Place the spring onions into the preserving jar, bulbs down, and wedge them in as firmly as possible. Pour the brine over until the onions are completely submerged and the brine is at least 2.5cm (1in) above them. Reserve any leftover brine. Cut a piece of yoghurt pot so that it is slightly larger than the diameter of the jar; this is called a follower. Bend the follower almost in half and slide it into the jar, wedging it on top of the vegetables so everything is submerged. If you need to add a weight to keep everything down, use a ziplock freezer bag filled with reserved brine.

Loosely close the jar (without the rubber seal) and leave to ferment at cool room temperature (19–20°C) for 3 days, then take out the weight and follower and drizzle in the honey and vinegar. Replace the follower and weight and leave to ferment for another 2 days.

The spring onions will start to look duller in colour and the brine will become cloudy. Test them after 5 days when they should have a sour, lightly vinegary flavour and pleasant crunch. There may be white scum on top of the brine, but this is harmless kahm yeast – just gently lift out the weight and follower and replace with clean ones if need be. When the spring onions are ready, replace the rubber seal and store in the fridge (with the follower in place) for up to 3 months, ensuring that the onions are always submerged in the brine. Open and reseal the jars once daily for the first few days of refrigeration to release any gas.

RADISH AND POMEGRANATE PICKLES

Makes about 200g (7oz)

Pomegranate molasses elevates the humble radish to a rosy, fragrant piquant thing that would tickle even the most jaded palate. Almost instant pickles! Taste as you go and add a little more salt or pomegranate molasses if your pickles don't taste as piquant as you would like. Because they are not fermented, you don't need to worry about getting the salt ratio right and your palate is the best guide.

Couple of handfuls of pink radishes, tops and tails left on, quartered

2–3 pinches of sea salt, to taste

1–2 tablespoons pomegranate molasses, to taste

Put the radishes, salt and pomegranate molasses into a bowl and mix together, then leave to macerate at room temperature for 3–6 hours. Stir every hour or so if you can, to ensure the radishes take up the flavour of the molasses. They should start to soften, give out some juice and turn a beautiful rose red colour. Eat as soon as they are rosy red.

Any you don't eat will keep for a couple of days in a lidded container in the fridge – pour in the juices too. Be aware that leftover radish pickles have the most amazing sulphurous pong, but they will still be good to eat for a couple of days despite this! Just open the window . . .

RADISH BOMBS

Makes 400g (14oz)

Every time I make these I am delighted by the transformation of bright red radishes to rose pink pickles. I like them fiery with chilli, ginger and garlic, hence the name, radish bombs, but they are equally good as a gentler pickle without chilli and ginger. Slice and adorn salads and stir fries, or munch as a pre-dinner snack to get your digestive juices flowing.

15g (½oz) sea salt

10g (¼oz) caster sugar

1 litre (1¾ pints) filtered or mineral water

3–4 pinches of dried chilli flakes

1–2 teaspoons seeds (either fennel, anise, cardamom, coriander or caraway seeds) or freshly ground black pepper, or 4–5 allspice berries (optional)

400g (14oz) radishes, tops trimmed

5 spring onions (white parts only), halved, or 1 red onion, sliced into rings

3–4 garlic cloves, halved

3 slices of fresh root ginger

2–3 large slices of lemon (cut from the middle of a lemon)

1-litre (1¾-pint) preserving jar without rubber seal

1 piece of yoghurt pot plastic to use as a follower or similar

Wash your preserving jar with hot, soapy water (no need to sterilise) and rinse well. Make the brine by stirring the salt and sugar into the water until dissolved. Sprinkle the chilli flakes and any seeds, black pepper or allspice berries (if using) into the preserving jar and then layer up the vegetables, garlic and ginger, finishing with the lemon slices on top.

Pour the brine over until everything is completely submerged and covered by at least 2.5cm (1in) and reserve any leftover brine. Wedge the follower on top (see Sweet Spring Onions recipe on page 206), making sure that everything is submerged. If you need to add a weight to keep everything down, use a ziplock freezer bag filled with reserved brine.

Loosely close the jar (without the rubber seal) and leave to ferment at cool room temperature (19–20°C) for 7–12 days. After 3–4 days, the radishes will magically lose their colour and the brine will turn pink. Taste them after 7 days to see if they are sour enough (a PH indicator strip will read between 3.2 and 4), but they may take up to 12 days to become properly sour. When they are ready, replace the rubber seal and store in the fridge for up to 6 months (making sure the radishes are submerged in the brine). Open and reseal the jars once daily for the first few days of refrigeration to release any gas.

RIBBON PICKLE

Makes 1 litre (1¾ pints)

This pickle is one of the best introductions to lacto-fermented vegetables. It's sweet, gingery and refreshing, with just enough sourness to make it tangy. Use as a relish, add it to salads for an instant bit of pep, or add to your stir fry off the heat to preserve the beneficial bacteria.

1kg (2¼lb) carrots, peeled

1 mouli radish, peeled, or handful of pink radishes, trimmed (optional)

Finely grated zest of ½ organic lemon (wash lemon in cold water first) (optional)

1 tablespoon peeled and finely grated fresh root ginger

8–15g (⅛–½oz) sea salt

2-litre (3½-pint) preserving jar
½ quantity of brine (page 198)
Smaller jars, for storage

Wash your preserving jar with hot, soapy water (no need to sterilise) and rinse well. Use a vegetable peeler to make long, thin strips from the carrots and mooli radish (if using). Thinly slice the pink radishes (if using). Put the prepared vegetables into a mixing bowl, then add the lemon zest (if using), ginger and 8g (⅛oz) of the salt.

Using clean hands, massage the ingredients together for 4–5 minutes, until the juices start to run. Taste for saltiness and decide whether you need to add any more; it should taste salty, but not unpleasantly so.

Pile into the preserving jar, pour in all the juices and press down with your fist or the end of a clean rolling pin until the juices rise to the top of the vegetables and cover them by about 1cm (½in). Place a ziplock freezer bag into the jar and pour enough brine into the bag so that it weighs the pickle down and the juices come up around the bag.

Zip up the bag, cover the open jar with a clean tea towel and leave to ferment at cool room temperature (19–20°C) for 5–7 days. Check the jar every day to see that the vegetables are submerged in brine and gasses are not building up below the weight. Taste after 5 days, when it should taste a little sour – sweet and sour really – if it's not sour enough, give it another day or two (a PH indicator strip will read between 3.2 and 4). When the pickle is ready, transfer to clean smaller jars, press down well and close up the jars. Store in the fridge and eat within a month. This ferment is more active because of the sugars in the carrots, so burp the jar every day for the first week in the fridge.

LABNEH

Makes about 500g (1lb 2oz)

Labneh is a fresh Middle-Eastern cheese made by hanging whole milk yoghurt in muslin until it is as thick as cream cheese, but with a tangy, slightly salty flavour. It is so quick to make and if you want to keep it for longer than a week, you can shape it into balls and submerge these in olive oil for a couple of months. Use it like feta in salads, dotted over a tray of roast vegetables, or to make my Toasted Buckwheat and Labneh Cheesecake (see page 96). Utterly delicious.

2 teaspoons fine sea salt

1kg (2¼lb) live Greek-style yoghurt

Large square of muslin

Stir the salt into the yoghurt. Line a mixing bowl with muslin and scrape the yoghurt into it, then tie up the corners of the muslin and suspend over the bowl, so that the whey can drip out. Leave at room temperature for 24 hours. I do this by hanging the muslin from the bars of a chair on the worktop, or by tying the muslin around a wooden spoon and placing this on top of a tall jug. You can also use a jelly bag with a frame, which looks much less Heath Robinson.

The labneh should have the texture of cream cheese after 24 hours and be firm enough to use for cheesecake or dips. If you would like to make Preserved Labneh (see page 211), transfer the labneh to the fridge and leave it to hang for another 24–36 hours, until it is more of a goats' cheese consistency and no whey is dripping out. Store in an airtight container in the fridge for up to a week. (Rinse and then boil your muslin cloth before washing it in the washing machine.)

GOATS' MILK LABNEH OR SHEEP'S MILK LABNEH

Substitute whole milk goats' milk or sheep's milk yoghurt for the Greek-style yoghurt in the recipe above. If you can buy goats' cream or sheep's cream, stir 100ml (3½fl oz) of this into the yoghurt for a richer labneh, as these yoghurts are thinner and lower in fat.

Line a mixing bowl as above, using two layers of muslin to prevent the thinner yoghurt running through the cloth, then scrape in the yoghurt, tie up the corners of the muslin and suspend over the bowl as before. Let the whey drip out for 24 hours at room temperature, and then for another 24 hours in the fridge. It may need a further 24 hours in the fridge to become firm enough to use for preserved labneh. Once it's ready, store in an airtight container in the fridge for up to a week.

PRESERVED LABNEH

Makes 1 litre (1¾ pints)

Fresh, creamy labneh cheese can be preserved by submerging it in olive oil to keep the air out and discourage aerobic bacteria that would like to eat the cheese before you get your hands on it. You can simply roll labneh into balls as it is, or cover them in a seed and spice mixture first for something intriguingly savoury. They are brilliant to have on hand for mezze and anti-pasti, or just squashed onto a piece of sourdough toast as a probiotic snack. Ensure you hang your labneh until it is really firm, as the reduced water content will help preserve it.

About 500ml (18fl oz) olive oil or extra-virgin olive oil, or cold-pressed rapeseed or sunflower oil

1 x quantity 36-hour Labneh recipe (see page 210)

2 bay leaves

Thinly pared long strips of rind from 1 lemon

3–4 thyme or oregano sprigs

Dukkah (see page 218), Gomasio (see page 214) or freshly chopped herbs, to serve (optional)

1-litre (1¾-pint) preserving jar

To sterilise the preserving jar, preheat the oven to 140°C/120°C fan/gas 1. Wash your preserving jar in warm, soapy water and rinse well. Remove the rubber seal, place the jar on a baking sheet and heat through in the oven for 20 minutes, then leave it to cool (you can use it as soon as it is cool). Pour boiling water over the seal and dry with kitchen paper before you fit it to the jar.

Oil your hands and scoop a teaspoon of the labneh into your palm. Roll into a ball and place into the sterilised preserving jar. Continue doing this (re-oiling your hands as necessary), until you have a layer of balls in the jar and then add a bay leaf, a couple of lemon rind strips or a herb sprig. Continue to fill up the jar this way with the remaining labneh, bay leaf, lemon rind and herb sprigs (alternating the aromatics as you go), until everything is used up, then pour the remaining oil over so that everything is submerged by about 2.5cm (1in). Give the jar a gentle shake to help everything settle and allow any air bubbles to travel up to the surface, then close up the jar.

The labneh will keep for a couple of months like this in the fridge. Ensure you use a clean utensil to take the labneh out of the jar (to avoid introducing bacteria), and top up the oil to ensure the labneh is always covered. You can eat the labneh balls just as they are, or roll them lightly in dukkah, gomasio or chopped herbs, just before serving, if you like.

SPRINKLED

GOMASIO

MIGAS

SHICHIMI TOGARASHI

DUKKAH

SPICY PUMPKIN SEEDS

SPICY CRUNCHY CHICKPEAS

For me, no meal is truly complete without some sort of crunchy sprinkle, whether I'm dipping my boiled egg into dukkah, or sprinkling migas into my soup – it's the crunchy, spicy bits that make my mouth water. Make a jar of everything here and sprinkle at will as they all contain beneficial ingredients that will make your meals more nutritious.

GOMASIO

Makes 90g (3½oz)

This delicious mixture of toasted sesame seeds, seaweed and salt is an umami-rich alternative to the salt and pepper pot. Both seaweed and sesame are said to promote a more alkaline environment in the body, making it less hospitable to bugs. Essential minerals, iodine and trace elements help to balance out the impact of salt on the body, so keep a pot on the table and sprinkle at will.

10g (¼oz) dried seaweed, such as dulse or wakame

75g (3oz) sesame seeds

½ teaspoon fennel seeds (optional)

1 teaspoon sea salt

Freshly ground black pepper, dried chilli flakes or smoked paprika (optional)

Preheat the oven to 180°C/160°C fan/gas 4. Put the seaweed on a baking sheet and bake for 10 minutes, until crispy. Set aside to cool.

Put the sesame and fennel seeds in a dry frying pan over a low heat and toast gently for 5–10 minutes, until tinged golden and starting to smell nutty. Spread out on a plate to cool.

Transfer the cooled seeds to a clean spice grinder or pestle and mortar with the seaweed and half of the salt and grind into a coarse powder. You may need to do this in batches. Add pepper, chilli flakes or smoked paprika to taste (if using) and as much of the remaining salt as you think it needs. It should taste reasonably salty.

Store the gomasio in an airtight container at room temperature for up to 2 weeks, or in the fridge for up to a month. Sprinkle over food to taste at the table.

VARIATIONS

NORI GOMASIO

Use 10g (¼oz) dried green or black nori flakes in place of dulse or wakame for a stronger flavoured gomasio. As the seaweed is already flaked, there is no need to bake it in the oven.

MIGAS

Makes 220g (8oz)

Migas means crumbs in Spanish, usually crumbs of bread fried until golden and used to improve almost anything. I mean, who doesn't love fried bread? In Spain and Portugal, migas can be padded out into a whole meal with meat, vegetables and lots of garlic, but I prefer to keep things simple, using them as a deliciously savoury addition to anything creamy, smooth or otherwise in need of crunch. They will go soft after a day, so just crisp them up in a pan if you have leftovers (you won't).

200g (7oz) sourdough bread without crusts

4 teaspoons duck, chicken or bacon fat or lard

Couple of pinches of sea salt

Freshly ground black pepper (optional)

Break the bread into very small pieces, none larger than your little fingernail. Heat the fat in a frying pan and fry the breadcrumbs over a highish heat, stirring often, until they are tinged golden and smell wonderful. Season with the salt and some black pepper, if you like, and sprinkle over your supper.

VARIATIONS

50g (2oz) black sesame seeds

2–3 teaspoons nigella seeds (optional)

200g (7oz) Migas (see above)

BLACK SESAME CRUMB (MAKES 270G/9½OZ)

Toast the sesame and nigella seeds (if using) in a dry frying pan over a medium heat for a few minutes, shaking the pan constantly, until they start to pop and smell nutty. Pour into a pestle and mortar, cool a little and then grind coarsely. Stir into the migas.

200g (7oz) Migas (see above)

3 rashers streaky bacon

1 tablespoon duck or chicken fat or lard

50g (2oz) roast peanuts, roughly chopped

PEANUT AND BACON CRUMB (MAKES 300G/11OZ)

Make the migas as before (you may not need to add any salt), but fry the bacon rashers in the fat first for about 5–6 minutes, until they are completely golden. Set aside to crisp up and then fry the bread pieces in the bacon fat. Finely chop the bacon and stir into the migas with the peanuts.

200g (7oz) Migas (see above)

1 garlic clove, very finely chopped

1½–2 teaspoons smoked paprika (optional)

100g (4oz) flaked almonds

GARLICKY ALMOND MIGAS (MAKES 300G/11OZ)

Make the migas as before, but when the breadcrumbs are almost done, add the garlic to the pan, turn the heat right down and cook gently, stirring all the time, until the garlic smells sweet (don't let it burn). Add the smoked paprika and toss to coat.

Toast the flaked almonds in a dry pan over a medium heat for about 6 minutes, stirring constantly, until the edges are tinged with gold and they smell sweetly nutty. Set aside to cool and then stir into the migas.

SHICHIMI TOGARASHI

Makes 50g (2oz)

This spicy sprinkle is perfect for bringing depth and heat to roasted meat, salty tempeh and even a plate of scrambled eggs. The components of shichimi togarashi can vary, but it is always made from seven ingredients that are chosen to bring the balance that is such an important part of Japanese food. It stimulates digestion, provides minerals and helps the liver to do its job, too. Although it is predominantly spicy, it also contains dried orange peel and seaweed, which give a bitter, sharp and savoury aspect that plain old chilli flakes just don't have. Put a bowlful on the table with meals.

1 tablespoon black or white sesame seeds

1 tablespoon black peppercorns

1 tablespoon dried clementine or orange peel

1 tablespoon dried chilli flakes

2 teaspoons white poppy seeds

2 teaspoons dried green or black nori flakes

2 teaspoons finely chopped fresh garlic

Toast the sesame seeds in a dry frying pan over a medium heat for a few minutes, shaking the pan regularly, until they start to smell nutty. Black sesame seeds won't change colour so take care not to burn them. Set aside to cool.

Using a pestle and mortar or spice grinder, grind the cooled sesame seeds with the black peppercorns, dried peel, chilli flakes and poppy seeds, until finely ground.

Stir in the nori flakes and garlic and put the mixture into a lidded jar. Store in the fridge for up to 6 weeks.

DUKKAH

Makes about 150g (5oz)

Dukkah is a spicy mixture of crushed or ground nuts, seeds and spices that is great for sprinkling over food, or dipping crunchy vegetables into. It's a particularly delicious way of getting some of those anti-inflammatory fats and spices into your diet and worth having a jar around to add a little extra depth to your meals.

FOR FENNEL SEED DUKKAH

150g (5oz) sunflower seeds

1 teaspoon fennel seeds

2 pinches of sea salt

1–2 pinches of chilli powder or dried chilli flakes

FOR PISTACHIO AND LINSEED DUKKAH

125g (4½oz) shelled pistachio nuts or blanched hazelnuts

4 teaspoons coriander seeds

1 teaspoon cumin seeds

1 teaspoon fennel seeds

4 tablespoons ground linseed

2–3 pinches of sea salt

For either dukkah, put either the sunflower and fennel seeds, or the pistachios or hazelnuts and coriander, cumin and fennel seeds, in a dry frying pan over a low heat and toast gently for 5–10 minutes, until tinged golden and starting to smell nutty (hazelnuts will take a little longer, so you might want to start them first and then add the spices 5 minutes or so later). Spread out on a plate to cool.

When the seeds or nuts and seeds are cool, roughly grind them into a coarse meal using a spice grinder or a pestle and mortar. You may need to do this in batches, and it is good if there is a little texture. Add the salt and chilli powder or chilli flakes to taste for the fennel seed dukkah, and add the ground linseed and salt to taste for the pistachio dukkah – each dukkah should taste salty as you are using it as a seasoning.

Store the dukkah in an airtight container at room temperature for up to 2 weeks, or in the fridge for up to a month.

Clockwise from top right:
Spicy Crunchy Chickpeas (see page 221), Spicy Pumpkin Seeds (see page 220), Migas (see page 215) and Pistachio and Linseed Dukkah (see above).

SPICY PUMPKIN SEEDS

Makes 200g (7oz)

Crunchy, spicy, savoury bits tickle our taste buds and stimulate the digestive system to do its job. These toasty seeds are perfect for sprinkling over salads, steamed broccoli and greens, or straight into your mouth as you cook supper. You can use sunflower seeds or even whole nuts, such as cashews, peanuts or almonds, instead, although the timings for the initial roast will need to be adjusted to suit.

200g (7oz) pumpkin seeds

1 teaspoon chilli powder or cayenne pepper

1 teaspoon smoked paprika

4 teaspoons tamari

Preheat the oven to 180°C/160°C fan/gas 4. Spread the pumpkin seeds out evenly on a baking sheet and roast for 6–8 minutes, until the seeds are starting to pop and crisp up. If they are soft at all, return to the oven for a few minutes more.

Combine the spices and tamari in a bowl. Add the hot seeds, turn to coat, then tip back onto the baking sheet and spread out evenly. Roast for another 3–4 minutes, until the seeds are dry and crisp again, but don't let them burn! The sugars in tamari burn quite quickly, so check after 2 minutes to be safe.

Cool completely on the baking sheet, then transfer whatever you and your family haven't scoffed immediately, into a lidded jar. They will keep for about a week at room temperature (if they go soft, just pop them back in the oven again for about 6–7 minutes, to crisp up).

SPICY CRUNCHY CHICKPEAS

Makes 300g (11oz)

Whether you need a little crunchy kick for a salad, or just fancy something moreish to nibble on with a glass of chilled dry sherry, these oven-baked chickpeas are unbeatably good. Packed with fibre as well as crunch, this is a snack that your microbes will go crazy for! Just don't eat the whole tray at once, unless you fancy a rather musical evening.

400g (14oz) tin chickpeas, rinsed and drained, or 200g (7oz) dried chickpeas

1 tablespoon chicken, bacon or duck fat, lard or coconut oil

1 heaped teaspoon cumin seeds

1 teaspoon paprika

2–3 pinches of chilli powder

2 pinches of sea salt

If you are using dried chickpeas, soak the chickpeas overnight in plenty of cold water. Drain the soaked chickpeas, then put into a pan and cover with fresh cold water. Bring to the boil and boil rapidly for 15 minutes, skimming off any froth that rises. Drain and rinse, return the chickpeas to the pan, cover with fresh water and bring to the boil again, then cover and simmer until tender, about 1½ hours. Drain and rinse, then set aside to cool.

Preheat the oven to 220°C/200°C fan/gas 7. Put the fat onto a baking tray and melt in the oven for a few minutes. Lay out some kitchen paper or a clean tea towel on another baking tray and tip the chickpeas onto it, then cover with more kitchen paper and roll the chickpeas around to dry them.

Take the tray out of the oven, tip the chickpeas onto it and shake the tray to coat them in the fat. Bake for 20–25 minutes, until the chickpeas are golden and crisp, giving the tray a shake halfway through baking.

While the chickpeas bake, toast the cumin seeds in a dry pan over a high heat for a couple of minutes, then tip into a pestle and mortar with the paprika, chilli powder and salt. Grind into a coarse powder and taste for chilli or salt, adding more, if you like.

When the chickpeas are done, tip them into a mixing bowl and add the spice mixture. Shake them well to coat, then set aside to cool before tucking in. The chickpeas will keep in an airtight container at room temperature for a week or so, but they will start to lose their crispness after a day or so.

DRESSED

TAHINI SAUCE

GARLIC OIL

VELVET DRESSING

CARAMELISED BUTTER

PROBIOTIC KETCHUP

Olive oil, tahini and butter are amongst the most delicious superfoods I know, enabling you to absorb the nutrients in vegetables, pulses and grains all the better. Dressings and sauces render meals far more satisfying, making it more likely that you will eat a good amount at meal times and avoid snacking through the day. Drizzle over salads, spoon into rice and daub onto your vegetables.

TAHINI SAUCE

Makes about 150ml (¼ pint)

Tahini is a loose paste made from sesame seeds. The flavour varies in bitterness and intensity depending on whether it is made with hulled sesame seeds and whether the seeds are toasted or not. My preference is for a lighter tahini. A fantastic source of absorbable calcium and other minerals, sesame is high in protein, fibre, anti-inflammatory fats and methionine (which supports liver function). Sesame loves dark greens, sweet roots, rich meats, fish and tempeh alike, so you may find yourself drizzling this creamy, garlicky sauce over any number of meals once you start.

2–3 garlic cloves
2 big pinches of sea salt
90g (3¼oz) tahini
Juice of 1 lemon

Crush the garlic into a paste with the salt – I use the flat side of a large knife or a pestle and mortar to do this. Stir in the tahini and lemon juice – the mixture will become stiff. Start to add cold water, a little at a time, and stir well between each addition to emulsify the mixture. Stop adding water when the sauce is the consistency of double cream. Check for salt, sour or garlic flavour and add more if you think it needs it.

Store the sauce in a lidded jar in the fridge for up to a week. Drizzle over steamed greens, lamb koftas, roast roots or crisp salads, or simply pour a little into a bowl for dipping raw vegetables into – great with a bowl of Dukkah (see page 218) to double dip (dip in tahini, then dukkah for a garlicky, spicy, crunch).

VARIATION

GREEN TAHINI SAUCE
In a blender, whizz the tahini sauce above with a big handful of flat-leaf parsley or coriander leaves for a bright green version that is particularly delicious with fish.

GARLIC OIL

Makes about 150ml (¼ pint)

The FODMAPs in garlic can present real problems for some people as they are much higher than in other members of the onion family. The fructans in garlic can be rendered more digestible by long, slow cooking, so this is one method of reducing the side effects of garlic – although it won't do anything for your garlic breath, so in order to neutralise that, eat something raw containing parsley, apple, pear or celeriac. Your ultimate goal should be to improve your gut health to a point where garlic does not present any problems, but in the meantime, this garlic oil gives the flavour of raw garlic to salad dressings and dips without the pain.

6 garlic cloves
150ml (¼ pint) olive oil

Lidded jar

Take the papery skins off the garlic, slice the cloves thinly and pop into the clean jar with the olive oil. Close up the jar and leave to macerate in the fridge for at least an hour, but ideally 6–8 hours. Do not leave it at room temperature for any longer than this, refrigerate if you need to leave it longer.

Strain out the garlic through a small sieve, then return the oil to the same jar and close up. Keep it in the fridge and use within a week.

VELVET DRESSING

Makes about 150ml (¼ pint)

This is my go-to dressing; silky smooth and deliciously sharp. I love a citronette made with lemon, but you could make a vinaigrette by using unpasteurised cider vinegar (this will be labelled as live, raw or 'with the mother') for a probiotic addition to the dressing. I generally make up a jar and keep it in the fridge, ready to shake and go when I'm having a salad. If you are eating low FODMAP, then you can still include the garlic, but might want to use just one clove. All of the oils listed are most beneficial eaten raw, so don't stint on the dressing!

2–3 garlic cloves, crushed (under a knife), or roughly sliced

1 teaspoon Dijon mustard

2 big pinches of sea salt

Juice of 1 lemon or 3 tablespoons raw (unpasteurised) cider vinegar

Extra-virgin olive oil or cold-pressed sunflower or rapeseed oil

Raw honey or pomegranate molasses (optional)

Smallish lidded jar

Put the garlic into the clean jar with the mustard, salt and lemon juice or vinegar. Pour in enough oil to 2–3 times the quantity of lemon juice, or 3–4 times the quantity of vinegar. You will be able to judge this by looking at the side of the jar, where the oil will float on the juice/vinegar.

Shake the jar vigorously until a creamy emulsion forms, then taste and adjust the seasoning, adding more oil, lemon juice or vinegar, salt, or a little honey or pomegranate molasses if it's too tart or your salad wants a little sweetness.

Close up the jar and store the dressing in the fridge for up to 3 days. Give it a good shake before serving.

CARAMELISED BUTTER

Makes 100g (4oz)

Butter takes on the most incredible nutty tones when you cook it so that the milk solids caramelise. I use this to bring an intense buttery kick to dal, eggs, soups and even vegetables. It is essentially the same as ghee or clarified butter, but I keep the flavoursome sediment that is usually discarded. Some people find ghee easier to digest than butter, because it is pure fat, with none of the irritating proteins. If you would like to make ghee, just strain the caramelised butter through a piece of muslin into a clean jar and discard the sediment. It will keep for at least a month in the fridge.

125g (4½oz) salted butter

Put the butter into a medium pan set over a medium heat and let it melt and then start to foam. Cook the butter, stirring frequently as it foams up and the liquid evaporates, leaving only the fat to bubble away.

When the butter is beginning to caramelise, you will notice a light golden brown colour come into the foam, and if you pull the pan off the heat and stir, the sediment in the bottom of the pan will start to turn golden and then golden brown. As soon as it looks golden brown, pour the butter into a waiting bowl to cool (sediment and all). Don't keep it in the pan a moment longer as it will burn quickly at this stage.

Use immediately or pour into a suitable lidded container and store in the fridge (it will keep for up to 3 weeks), then re-warm the amount that your recipe calls for.

VARIATION

SMOKY BUTTER
Simply stir 1–2 teaspoons smoked paprika into the cooked butter, according to your taste. It will turn a beautiful brick red colour.

PROBIOTIC KETCHUP

Makes about 500g (1lb 2oz)

If you despair because someone you love covers everything they eat in commercial ketchup, help is at hand! If you love a sweet and sour sauce, but don't want to pile all that sugar on your plate, this is the one for you. I see a relish as an opportunity to get some friendly bacteria on board, so this simple intro to fermenting is just perfect. I can't think of many things it wouldn't improve, but my top favourite is to dip crispy Panelle (see page 185) into a generous portion and eat them in the last rays of sun. Heaven.

4 tablespoons olive oil

1 carrot, diced

½ celery stick, diced

75g (3oz) shallots, chopped

60g (2¼oz) dried stoned dates, chopped

2 pinches of ground allspice

1 bay leaf

1 teaspoon sea salt

400g (14oz) passata

50ml (2fl oz) whey from Labneh (see page 210)

1-litre (1¾-pint) preserving jar

½ quantity of brine (see page 198)

Smaller jars, for storage

Heat the olive oil in a pan, add the carrot, celery and shallots and sauté very gently for about 20 minutes, stirring occasionally, until the vegetables are soft, sweet and just starting to colour. Add the dates, allspice, bay leaf, salt and passata to the pan, turn up the heat and cook, uncovered, stirring occasionally, until the mixture is thicker and sweet smelling and the veg are completely soft. Cool completely, then fish out the bay leaf.

Wash your preserving jar with hot, soapy water (no need to sterilise) and rinse well. Put the cooled passata mixture into a blender with the whey and blend until completely smooth. Scrape into your preserving jar and tuck an open ziplock freezer bag on top. Pour enough brine into the freezer bag so that it will act as a weight and keep the air out of the jar. Zip up the bag, but do not close the jar. Cover with a clean tea towel and leave to ferment (out of direct sunlight) at cool room temperature (19–20°C) for about 48 hours, but check it sooner if the temperature is warm. The ketchup should taste slightly more sour than when it went in the jar but not fizzy.

When the ketchup is ready, decant it into clean smaller jars and close up, then store in the fridge and eat within 2 weeks. The ketchup will continue to ferment in the fridge, so keep an eye on it. Open and reseal the jars once daily for the first few days of refrigeration to release any gas. If it has a little fizz, then it's still fine to eat, but if it's climbing out of the jar, you may want to feed it to the compost.

DRINKS & TONICS

FRESH TURMERIC AND ROSE TEA

FENNEL, STAR ANISE AND LIQUORICE TEA

FRESH HERB TEAS

BUCKWHEAT TEA (SOBA-CHA)

AFTER-DINNER CACAO TEA

ALMOND MILK

WATER KEFIR

PINK PLUM KEFIR

GINGER BEER KEFIR

SUNFLOWER SEED CREAM

BEET KVASS

RHUBARB AND ROSE FIZZ

DIGESTIVE BITTERS

While there is nothing inherently wrong with caffeine, it can be good to have a break from it from time to time, and some of us are more sensitive to it than others. If you have been put off herbal teas by those awful scented teabags that promise a tropical fruit bowl and taste of pot-pourri, try cradling a mug of one of these freshly made herb teas instead.

Treat yourself to some Iranian rose water and seek out some fresh turmeric root for a tea that is subtle, soothing and restorative, or nix your craving for cake with a cup of rich cacao nib tea.

Water kefir and beet kvass make wonderful probiotic and mineral-rich additions to your diet, and digestive bitters are brilliant for helping a sluggish digestive system to wake up and supporting an overworked liver. Everything here is a delicious and healing addition to your diet, whether your body is seeking calm or nourishment.

FRESH TURMERIC AND ROSE TEA

Makes a pot for 2

The excitement surrounding turmeric in the press might lead you to believe that it is a miraculous cure-all, and while it is highly antioxidant and anti-inflammatory, it's always worth bearing in mind that a varied diet will do far more to ensure your longevity. Dried turmeric can have a distinctly bitter and musty flavour, but the fresh root is fragrant and floral with no bitterness at all. This is my favourite tea to start the day with and as turmeric supports liver function, the morning is an ideal time to drink it, although it can also be an excellent after-dinner drink if you suffer from indigestion or struggle to digest fats.

Thumb-sized piece of fresh turmeric root

Freshly boiled water

Good grind of black pepper

1–2 teaspoons rose water

Raw honey (optional)

Slice the turmeric root thinly, either wearing gloves or using a fork to steady it if you are worried about staining your fingers. Put it into a teapot and cover with a couple of cups of freshly boiled water. Let the tea brew for 4 minutes and then add the black pepper, and rose water to taste.

Pour into cups through a tea strainer and sweeten with a little honey, if you like. Keep the turmeric root as you can use it to brew up another pot of tea – just muddle it a little with the end of a rolling pin first.

FENNEL, STAR ANISE AND LIQUORICE TEA

Makes a pot for 2

Naturally sweet liquorice root is very soothing for the digestive tract, it aids blood sugar regulation and can reduce sugar cravings. It is also an adaptogenic herb that your body can use to manufacture adrenal hormones and support adrenal function through stressful periods. One caution with liquorice root is that it can raise blood pressure if taken in excess, but a couple of cups a day is a completely safe amount. Fennel and all aniseedy plants have a soothing effect on the digestive tract, making them a traditional choice for digestif drinks after supper.

1 teaspoon fennel seeds (or anise seeds)

1 liquorice root teabag (or 1 heaped teaspoon liquorice root powder)

2 star anise

Freshly boiled water

Warm the teapot with hot water and empty out. Bruise the fennel seeds using a pestle and mortar, then add them to the teapot with the teabag and star anise and cover with recently boiled water.

Allow to steep for 5 minutes, then pour into cups through a tea strainer. If you like, fish out the star anise and float one on top of each cup of tea.

FRESH HERB TEAS

Makes a pot for 2

As well as adding as many herbs to your diet as possible, think about growing a few for the teapot. There are many delicious mints, lemony herbs and sweet flowering herbs that are easy to grow in a garden or even a window box. Just think of the wonderful soil bacteria you will get every time you make a cup of tea! Below are some suggestions based on teas that I like, but the possibilities are endless. Use 1–2 large handfuls of herbs per pot, depending on the strength of the herb flavour – strong herbs like sage, thyme, bay and rosemary need only a small handful.

SOOTHING HERBS
Chamomile flowers, lemon balm, lemon verbena, fennel tops, sweet cicely leaves and seeds, meadowsweet flowers, borage leaves and flowers, gorse blossom, rose petals

STIMULATING HERBS
Mint (especially Moroccan mint, chocolate mint, ginger mint and liquorice mint), sage, thyme, rosemary, bay leaf

DELICIOUS ADDITIONS (OPTIONAL)
Cinnamon stick (dry out and re-use), pared citrus rind, rose water, orange flower water (use sparingly), Digestive Bitters (1 teaspoon max) (see page 246)

Recently boiled water
Raw honey or date syrup, to sweeten

Warm the teapot first with hot water and empty out. Bruise your chosen herbs by crushing them gently between your palms, then pop them into the teapot (with a cinnamon stick or some citrus rind, if using), then cover with a couple of cups of recently boiled water.

Leave to steep for 5 minutes, then pour into cups through a tea strainer. Stir in rose or orange flower water or digestive bitters (if using). Sweeten with a little honey or date syrup, if you like, but aim not to.

BUCKWHEAT TEA (SOBA-CHA)

Makes enough tea for at least 20 servings

In Japan, roast buckwheat groats are used to make a delicious tea that is reputed to improve circulation and help balance blood sugar due to its rutin content. Black or tartary buckwheat is much higher in rutin than the common buckwheat we eat, so look out for this in an apothecary or Japanese food supplier, or buy black buckwheat tea ready-made. I love the flavour of tea made with plain old roasted buckwheat and this is what I tend to use, knowing that I already eat lots of antioxidants in my plant-heavy diet. It has a nutty, slightly tannic, floral quality that is refreshing without milk and comforting with it.

150g (5oz) buckwheat groats

Recently boiled water

Milk and raw honey, to serve (optional)

Put the buckwheat groats into a dry frying pan and toast gently over a medium heat for about 10 minutes, stirring frequently. They should turn a reddish brown colour and smell very toasty, but don't let them catch too much or the tea will taste very bitter. Set aside to cool and then store in an airtight container for up to a month.

To make the tea, warm the teapot first with hot water and empty out. Put a heaped tablespoon of the toasted buckwheat groats per person into the teapot and cover with recently boiled water. Leave to brew for 5 minutes and then pour into cups through a tea strainer.

Drink black or add a splash of milk (almond or rice milk is my favourite) and a small spoonful of honey if you like, turning the tea from golden brown to peach pink.

AFTER-DINNER CACAO TEA

Makes a pot for 2

When cocoa is roasted it loses many of the antioxidant benefits that the raw bean contains, so this delicious tea is a good anti-inflammatory choice when you fancy a little something chocolatey. Sweeten it if you like, but you can also enjoy the bitter cocoa flavours, knowing that they will be stimulating your liver to work better.

2 tablespoons raw cacao nibs
1 teaspoon vanilla extract
Tiny pinch of ground nutmeg
Grind of black pepper
Recently boiled water
Date syrup, to taste (optional)

Warm your teapot with hot water and empty out. Put the cacao nibs, vanilla extract, nutmeg and black pepper into the teapot and cover with two cups of recently boiled water. Leave to steep for 5 minutes, then pour into cups through a tea strainer. Sweeten to taste with date syrup, if you like.

You can make another batch with the same cacao nibs as long as you do it within 24 hours (just leave them in the teapot or tip them into a bowl and cover, ready to use later).

When you have finished using the nibs for tea, store them in the fridge in an airtight container (for up to 3 days) and add them to smoothies, porridge or yoghurt. The tea making softens them, so they make a deliciously chocolatey addition to your meals.

ALMOND MILK

Makes 1 litre (1¾ pints)

I like my rooibos tea with almond milk, it has a wonderful creamy flavour and contains none of the emulsifiers that commercial nut milks tend to. Try heating a cupful with a little ground cinnamon and nutmeg for a delicious and comforting bedtime drink, a little like Mexican Horchata. Milks can also be made in the same way using any other nuts or seeds, although they do vary in their creaminess. See the Sunflower Seed Cream recipe that follows (page 243) for a dairy-free alternative to cream.

100g (4oz) whole almonds

900ml (1½ pints) filtered or mineral water

Pinch of sea salt

1–2 teaspoons date or maple syrup or raw honey (optional)

½ teaspoon vanilla extract (optional)

If you do not have a powerful blender, you may find that you need to strain the almond milk through fine muslin to get it completely smooth. You can use the leftover nut pulp in muesli or for bread-making.

Put the almonds into a heatproof bowl and cover with boiling water from the kettle. Leave to soak until the nuts are cool enough to handle, then drain and pop them out of their jackets, one by one. Alternatively, use blanched almonds and soak them in cold water for a couple of hours first. Discard the soaking water.

Put the naked almonds into your blender (or food-processor) with 200ml (7fl oz) of the measured water and blend until they are very finely ground and looking like porridge. Add the salt, syrup or honey (if using), vanilla extract (if using) and most of the remaining water, then blend again until the mixture looks smooth and creamy. Add the remaining water plus extra if you think it needs thinning down a little.

Pour into a suitable airtight container and keep it in the fridge. Unsweetened nut milk should keep in the fridge for up to 5 days, but if it is sweetened, use within 3 days or it may start to ferment.

WATER KEFIR

Makes 1 litre (1¾ pints)

Water kefir grains are a type of SCOBY (symbiotic community of bacteria and yeast) that feed on sugar water, making a delicious probiotic drink in the process. Depending on what you flavour it with post fermentation, water kefir can taste like lemonade, ginger beer or fruit squash – albeit tarter versions of these. If you bottle the drink and leave it to ferment for another 12–24 hours, it will carbonate naturally into a delicious, sparkling pick-me-up.

3 tablespoons sugar (about 50–70g/2–2½oz) (see Notes on page 240 on type to use)

1 litre (1¾ pints) filtered or mineral water (chlorinated tap water will kill the kefir grains)

2 heaped tablespoons kefir grains

1 slice from an organic lemon

Couple of pieces of organic dried fruit, such as figs, unsulphured apricots or prunes

1.5-litre (2½-pint) Kilner jar or other preserving jar

Stoppered or screw top glass bottles, for storage (don't use plastic bottles)

Wash your Kilner or preserving jar with hot, soapy water (no need to sterilise) and rinse well. Stir the sugar into the water until dissolved, then pour into the Kilner or preserving jar. Add the kefir grains, lemon slice and chosen dried fruit and give it a stir with a wooden spoon, then close up the jar. If your jar has a rubber seal, remove this so that gases don't build up. (If you can't find an organic lemon, try adding a few drops of cider vinegar to your first batch of kefir and then leave some liquid in the jar when you strain it (once it has fermented). This is done to keep the PH low.)

Leave to ferment at room temperature for 24–48 hours, until the kefir tastes sourish. The more sour it is, the less sugar and more of the beneficial lactic and acetic acids it will contain. I usually give mine 48 hours. Don't give it longer than 48 hours at this stage or the grains will start to suffer.

When it is ready to bottle, discard the lemon slice and dried fruit. Strain the water kefir and grains through a sieve, reserve the grains (see page 240) and pour the water kefir into clean stoppered or screw top glass bottles, leaving a little space at the top of each, then close the stoppers or screw on the tops. You can now leave the kefir at room temperature for 12–24 hours to carbonate, depending on how potent it is. Check the fizziness by burping each bottle (undo stopper or lid to release any gas that has built up) every 4 hours or so – don't let them over-carbonate or the bottles could explode! Put them into the fridge once they have carbonated enough, as this will slow the fermentation. The kefir will keep in the fridge for about a week.

Start by having a small glassful of water kefir a couple of times a day and then increase the amount you drink over a week, up to however much you like. Go slowly at first as the probiotic can sometimes make people bloated and has a cleansing action on the liver in some. If you don't have any digestive issues, you can probably drink as much as you like right away.

Use the kefir grains to make your next batch of water kefir as before and drink the batch you have made. Your kefir grains need to be fed every couple of days this way if they are to thrive. You don't need to wash the grains, nor the jar between batches, unless you see frothy scum developing around the inside of the jar. If this happens, just rinse the grains in fresh filtered or mineral water, wash the jar and continue as usual. Your grains will last for years if they are happy and well fed.

If you are going away or need a break from your grains, make a solution of 500ml (18fl oz) filtered or mineral water and 35g (1¼oz) sugar, put the grains into a clean 1-litre (1¾-pint) glass jar, add a slice of lemon and a dried unsulphured apricot (or dried fig or prune) and fill with the sugar solution. Put the container in the fridge straight away. They should be ok for up to 2 weeks like this, possibly a little longer. If the liquid becomes too acidic they will start to pickle in it. When you wake them up from the cold again (drain them, discarding the sugar water, lemon and dried fruit), they may be a bit sluggish and take an extra day to brew.

NOTES

Your grains need lots of calcium, so every 2–3 weeks I add an eggshell to the initial ferment. Cover the eggshell in boiling water and when it is cool enough to handle, remove the membrane inside, then add the eggshell to your grains in the jar.

You can also vary the type of sugar you use (to vary the nutrients the grains get), from white to the darkest muscovado, or even maple syrup or molasses, but I mostly stick to white sugar as darker sugars can make the kefir a bit yeasty.

Your grains should increase after a couple of weeks – this means they are happy. Stick to the quantity of grains given in the recipe and store any extra as detailed above. You can eat them in muesli to get a super probiotic effect, or give them away once you have enough extra.

PINK PLUM KEFIR

Makes 1 litre (1¾ pints)

If you use the dark red-skinned plums for this kefir it will turn a wonderful shade of candy pink. All plums, or even greengages, work here, but really ripe plums make something that is a little like a fragrant cream soda with those floral notes that plums sometimes have. It is the most wonderful sparkling pick-me-up on a summer's day.

1 litre (1¾ pints) Water Kefir (48 hours fermented) (see page 239)

6 dark-skinned plums, stoned and chopped

1 tablespoon caster sugar

2-litre (3½-pint) Kilner jar or mixing bowl to macerate the rhubarb

Piece of muslin and a sieve

Stoppered or screw top glass bottles, to carbonate (don't use plastic bottles)

Pour the water kefir into the clean Kilner jar or mixing bowl, add the plums and sugar and stir, then close up the jar without the rubber seal or cover the bowl, and leave to macerate at room temperature for 6–8 hours.

When it's ready, strain the plum kefir through a muslin-lined sieve. This removes any plum debris that will make the kefir fizz out of the bottle when you carbonate it. Pour the strained kefir into clean stoppered or screw top glass bottles, leaving at least 5cm (2in) or so of space at the top of each, then close the stoppers or screw on the tops. Leave at room temperature for 12–24 hours. Burp each bottle every 4 hours by gently releasing the stopper or screw top to see how much gas comes out – if you get a little sigh, give it another 6–12 hours, but if you get a whoosh, or the kefir starts to fizz up in the bottle, quickly tighten the stopper or screw top and put the bottle in the fridge. Chilling will calm the carbonation down a little.

You can drink the kefir straight away or it will keep in the fridge for up to a week. It will become a little sourer each day as the bacteria slowly consume the remaining sugar.

GINGER BEER KEFIR

Makes 1 litre (1¾ pints)

There's something about ginger beer that feels really restorative and this is my choice of pick-me-up, whether I'm feeling tired and under the weather, or have just got back from an exhilarating run. Ginger is fantastic for any kind of nausea and is calming and supportive for the digestive system. Dried ginger gives a delicious warmth to the drink, but you must steep it in muslin or the particles will make the ginger beer so explosive that your drink may leap out of the bottle before it gets a chance to touch your lips!

1 litre (1¾ pints) Water Kefir (48 hours fermented) (see page 239)

½ teaspoon ground ginger

1½ teaspoons grated fresh root ginger

1½ teaspoons date syrup

Piece of muslin, kitchen string and a sieve

Stoppered or screw top glass bottles, to carbonate (don't use plastic bottles)

Pour the water kefir into a mixing bowl or jug. Fold the muslin double and tip the ground ginger into it, then tie securely into a bundle with the string, making sure that none of the ginger can leak out. Pop the muslin bundle into the kefir, cover and leave to macerate at room temperature for a couple of hours.

Remove the muslin and squeeze it into the kefir. Squeeze the juice from the grated ginger into the kefir through a sieve, stir in the date syrup and check that the kefir tastes gingery enough.

Pour the strained kefir into clean stoppered or screw top glass bottles, leaving at least 5cm (2in) or so of space at the top of each, then close the stoppers or screw on the tops. Leave at room temperature for 6–12 hours. Burp each bottle every 4 hours by gently releasing the stopper or screw top to see how much gas comes out – if you get a little sigh, give it another few hours, but if you get a whoosh, or the kefir starts to fizz up in the bottle, quickly tighten the stopper or screw top and put the bottle in the fridge. Chilling will calm the carbonation down a little.

You can drink the kefir straight away or it will keep in the fridge for up to a week. It will become a little sourer each day as the bacteria slowly consume the remaining sugar.

SUNFLOWER SEED CREAM

Makes 200ml (7fl oz)

This cream is delicious spooned over fruit, or left unsweetened it can be used much like tahini sauce. Cashew nuts, pecans, pistachio nuts and macadamia nuts also make delicious creams.

50g (2oz) sunflower seeds

Pinch of sea salt

1–2 teaspoons date or maple syrup or raw honey (optional)

1 teaspoon vanilla extract (optional)

Put the sunflower seeds in a dry frying pan over a low heat and toast gently, shaking the pan regularly, for about 10 minutes, until they are lightly golden. Transfer to a bowl, pour over 150ml (¼ pint) cold water and leave to soak for an hour. Transfer the seeds and soaking water to a food-processor and process until smooth. Add the salt, syrup or honey (if using) and vanilla extract (if using), then process again, adding a little extra cold water if necessary, until the mixture looks like thick, unwhipped double cream. Pour into a clean lidded jar and store in the fridge for up to 5 days if unsweetened, and up to 3 days if sweetened.

BEET KVASS

Makes 1 litre (1¾ pints)

This probiotic, mineral-rich drink has a sour, earthy flavour that can be an acquired taste, but once you get accustomed to a slightly salty drink you might find you crave it as a pick-me-up. You can leave it to carbonate in a bottle for a fizzier kvass, or let it get very sour in the jar for instant pink pickles and adding a sharp kick to soups.

4–5 small or 2–3 large raw beetroot (about 700–800g/1lb 9oz–1¾lb total), well-scrubbed, trimmed and chopped into 1cm (½in) dice

1 teaspoon sea salt

125ml (4fl oz) live natural yoghurt whey (see Labneh recipe on page 210) or Water Kefir (see page 239) (optional)

About 1 litre (1¾ pints) filtered or mineral water

2-litre (3½-pint) preserving jar
Stoppered or screw top glass bottles, for storage

Wash your preserving jar with hot, soapy water (no need to sterilise) and rinse well. Place the chopped beetroot in the preserving jar with the salt, whey or water kefir (if using) and enough water to fill the jar, leaving at least 2.5cm (1in) at the top for expansion. Take the rubber seal out of the jar if it has one.

Close up the jar and leave to ferment at cool room temperature (18–20°C) for 7–10 days until it tastes strongly of beetroot, is a deep purple red colour and tastes more salty and sour than earthy and sweet. It may develop a little harmless white scum on the top (kahm yeast), just skim it off and place a piece of baking parchment on the surface. Strain the liquid through a sieve and pour into clean stoppered or screw top glass bottles, leaving a little space at the top of each, then close the stoppers or screw on the tops. Once you strain off the beets, you can leave the liquid to ferment in the bottles at cool room temperature for a further 3–7 days to get more sour and a little fizzy – just remember to burp each bottle regularly (undo stopper or lid to release any gas that has built up) and keep checking the sourness. Refrigerate, once it is as sour as you would like.

Kvass will keep in the fridge for at least 3–4 weeks. You can drink it neat, or half and half with fizzy water. You can add a little raw honey to your glass – but not to the bottle as the natural yeasts may ferment the sugar into alcohol.

CARROT AND GINGER KVASS

For a lighter kvass, try using the same quantity of carrots, peeled and diced, instead of beetroot. For a little tummy settling kick, add a thumb-sized piece of fresh root ginger (about 60g/2¼oz), sliced into coins, to the carrots. This ferment can be more gassy, so burp the jar daily.

RHUBARB AND ROSE FIZZ

Makes 1 litre (1¾ pints)

When the rhubarb arrives in February it seems like the essence of spring. I fall upon it hungrily, knowing I can soon drink a bubbly glass of spring-scented fizz, even if the weather is cold and damp.

1 litre (1¾ pints) Water Kefir (48 hours fermented) (see page 239)

250g (9oz) pink rhubarb, trimmed and chopped into small dice

1 tablespoon caster sugar

Few drops of beetroot juice or Beet Kvass (see page 244) (optional)

Few drops of rose water (such as Cortas brand), or to taste

2-litre (3½-pint) Kilner jar or mixing bowl to macerate the rhubarb

Piece of muslin and a sieve

Stoppered or screw top glass bottles, to carbonate (don't use plastic bottles)

Pour the water kefir into the clean Kilner jar or mixing bowl, add the rhubarb and sugar and stir, then close up the jar without the rubber seal or cover the bowl, and leave to macerate at room temperature for about 10 hours.

When it's ready, strain the rhubarb kefir through a muslin-lined sieve. This removes any rhubarb debris that will make the kefir fizz out of the bottle when you carbonate it. Although the kefir will be a gorgeous rose pink at this point, it will lose its colour in a matter of hours, so you can add a little beetroot juice or beet kvass to keep it pink, if you like. Add a few drops of rose water to taste – I love rose, so I would go for a couple of teaspoonfuls, but rose water varies in strength, so go cautiously.

Pour the strained kefir into clean stoppered or screw top glass bottles, leaving at least 5cm (2in) or so of space at the top of each, then close the stoppers or screw on the tops. Leave at room temperature for 8–12 hours. Burp each bottle every 4 hours by gently releasing the stopper or screw top to see how much gas comes out – if you get a little sigh, give it another few hours, but if you get a whoosh, or the kefir starts to fizz up in the bottle, quickly tighten the stopper or screw top and put the bottle in the fridge. Chilling will calm the carbonation down a little.

You can drink the kefir straight away or it will keep in the fridge for up to a week. It will become a little sourer each day as the bacteria slowly consume the remaining sugar.

DIGESTIVE BITTERS

Makes about 175ml (6fl oz)

Bitter things stimulate the liver to produce bile, helping you digest and absorb the fats you eat. Digestive bitters have long been used to calm and support the gut, and they often contain other therapeutic ingredients that settle or stimulate the whole digestive tract and support other organs along the way. You can take a teaspoon on the tongue before meals, or a couple of teaspoons in a small glass of sparkling water makes a fantastic aperitif or digestif. Check out the Useful Suppliers (see page 248) for ingredients that don't come from the hedgerow or your garden.

FOR THE PLUM OR APPLE BITTERS

4–5 plums, stoned and chopped, or 2 sweet eating apples, chopped

1 tablespoon vanilla extract (optional)

½ teaspoon dried gentian root, or 2 fresh dandelion roots, scrubbed and sliced into coins

1 teaspoon dried angelica root (optional)

2 cloves

200ml (7fl oz) vodka

Raw honey, to taste

FOR THE HEDGEROW BITTERS

60g (2¼oz) fully ripe fresh elderberries

50g (2oz) fresh blackberries

25g (1oz) fresh sloes, pricked all over with a toothpick

½ teaspoon dried gentian root, or 2 fresh dandelion roots, scrubbed and sliced into coins

200ml (7fl oz) vodka

Raw honey, to taste

FOR THE CHOCOLATE BITTERS

50g (2oz) raw cacao nibs

2 split vanilla pods or 2 tablespoons vanilla extract

¼ teaspoon dried mace pieces or a pinch of ground mace (optional)

½ teaspoon dried gentian root, or 2 fresh dandelion roots, scrubbed and sliced into coins

200ml (7fl oz) vodka

Date syrup, to taste

Large jam jar

Smaller jam jar, for storage

Wash your larger jam jar with hot, soapy water (no need to sterilise) and rinse well. Gather all your aromatic ingredients (including the fruit or cacao nibs) and place them in the jam jar. Pour in the vodka to cover them, but leave out the honey or date syrup, as this is added later. Close up the jar, put into a dark, cool place and leave for 3–6 weeks, shaking a little and tasting at weekly intervals after the first couple of weeks to decide whether the flavour is bitter and aromatic enough for you.

When the bitters taste fragrant, bitter and mellow, strain out the aromatics through a tea strainer or muslin-lined sieve. Stir in enough sweetener to just take the edge off the bitterness and round out the flavours of the aromatics, or leave as they are – they must taste bitter in order to stimulate your liver. Pour into a clean, smaller jam jar and close up. Store at room temperature.

The bitters should keep for at least 6 months, but the flavours can change, so keep testing them – and using them!

USEFUL SUPPLIERS

Abel & Cole
(https://www.abelandcole.co.uk)
Online suppliers of organic and ethically sourced food including: charcuterie, Guernsey milk and yoghurt, meat, fish and veg boxes, milk kefir, sausages, sourdough bread and stock bones.

Arctic Power Berries
(www.arcticpowerberries.com)
Berry powders including: blackcurrant, blueberry, lingonberry and sea buckthorn.

Baldwins
(https://www.baldwins.co.uk)
A specialist herbalist supplier of a huge range of herbs and aromatics including: angelica root, burdock root, dandelion root, digestive bitters, dried citrus peels, gentian root and spices. Available online or visit the lovely old-fashioned shop on the Walworth Road in London.

Bare Naked Foods
(https://www.barenakedfoods.co.uk)
Supply konjac (shirataki) noodles and konjac 'rice'; also available in many supermarkets.

Cornish Seaweed Company
(www.cornishseaweed.co.uk)
A lovely range of hand collected seaweeds, from kombucha and dulse to sea salad and seaweed salts. Available in a range of shops and online.

Eversfield Organic
(https://www.eversfieldorganic.co.uk)
A fantastic Devon-based supplier of organic meats and charcuterie, rare breeds, offal, stock bones, bone broth, beef fat, Guernsey milk yoghurt (Brown Cow Organics) and meat and veg boxes, including a paleo box and wild game box.

Fresh Tempeh
(www.freshtempeh.co.uk)
A small company making fresh tempeh for mail order.

Fushi
(https://www.fushi.co.uk)
Cold-pressed oils including: almond, argan, avocado, coconut, peanut, sesame and sunflower. Also grass-fed ghee. Available direct, from selected health food retailers or from Ocado (https://www.ocado.com).

Green Pasture Farms
(www.greenpasturefarms.co.uk)
A farming collective in Lancashire supplying grass-fed meats, rusk-free sausages, offal, stock bones, fats and meat boxes.

Healthy Supplies
(www.healthysupplies.co.uk)
Online supplier of a vast array of whole food ingredients including seaweeds, teff grain, whole oats and gluten-free flours.

Happy Kombucha
(https://happykombucha.co.uk)
A veritable fermenting goldmine! Ginger beer plants, kombucha mothers, milk kefir grains, sourdough starters, tempeh starters, water kefir grains and yoghurt starters. Fermenting kits for kefir, kombucha and vegetables, natural salt for fermenting, plus lots of useful information, guides and troubleshooting articles on the whole subject of fermentation.

Hodmedods
(https://hodmedods.co.uk)
A farming collective supplying British-grown quinoa, pulses, pulse flours such as fava bean, yellow pea and green pea, puffed quinoa and roasted bean snacks.

Impulse Foods

(www.impulsefoods.co.uk)
Succulent frozen tempeh made in Somerset and available in many health food shops and online health food retailers.

Melbury & Appleton

(www.melburyandappleton.co.uk)
An online delicatessen selling a huge range of world food ingredients including: barberries, carob molasses, Cortas orange flower water, Cortas rosewater, date syrup, dried cherries, ghee, kombu, moong dal, pomegranate molasses and preserved lemons.

Riverford Organic Farmers

(https://www.riverford.co.uk)
Devon-based online suppliers of 100 per cent organic veg and meat boxes containing ingredients sourced from small-scale organic producers and delivered around the whole of the UK. Meat boxes can include offal and stock bones.

Shipton Mill

(www.shipton-mill.com)
A fantastic mill with an amazing range of flours, from their gluten-free range produced in a dedicated mill (brown rice flour, buckwheat flour, chestnut flour, gram flour, millet flour, oat flour, quinoa flour and teff flour) to their organic ancient grain flours (einkorn, emmer and Khorasan) and range of rye and spelt flours. They also sell delicious organic fresh yeast.

Sous Chef

(www.souschef.co.uk)
An online delicatessen with a dizzying array of world food and exotic ingredients including: barberries, berry powders, black rice, buckwheat groats, cacao nibs, chestnut flour, coarse grey sea salt, coconut oil, cold-pressed oils, Cortas orange flower water, Cortas rosewater, date syrup, dried cherries, dried orange peel, duck fat, freeze-dried berries, ghee, goose fat, pomegranate molasses, preserved lemons, saffron, seaweeds, teff flour and grain, unpasteurised cider vinegar, white, black and red quinoa.

Tideford Organics

(www.tidefordorganics.com)
A delicious range of miso made in Totnes, Devon. Available from health food shops, some supermarkets and online suppliers.

Tobia Teff

(www.tobiateff.co.uk)
Online supplier of teff flour, teff bread and cereals.

Whole Foods Market

(www.wholefoodsmarket.com)
A whole food supermarket with branches in London, Cheltenham and Glasgow, selling a huge range of grains, pulses, seaweeds, gluten-free flours and organic produce. It is also worth approaching your local health food shop to see if they can order products for you.

Yu & Mi

(https://yuandmicompany.com)
Suppliers of dried shirataki noodles and konjac 'rice' with a little more bite than many pre-soaked shirataki noodles.

INDEX

First published in 2017
by HEADLINE PUBLISHING GROUP

1

Cataloguing in Publication Data is available from the British Library

Hardback ISBN 978 1 4722 4511 3
eISBN 978 1 4722 4512 0

Commissioning Editor: Muna Reyal
Project Editor: Kate Miles
Illustrations: Ana Zaja Petrak
Photography: Laura Edwards
Design and Art Direction: Miranda Harvey
Home Economist: Aya Nishimura
Prop Stylist: Tabitha Hawkins
Copy Editor: Anne Sheasby
Proofreader: Margaret Gilbey
Indexer: Caroline Wilding

Colour origination by Born Group
Printed and bound in Germany by Mohn Media

HEADLINE PUBLISHING GROUP
An Hachette UK Company
Carmelite House
50 Victoria Embankment
London EC4Y 0DZ

www.headline.co.uk
www.hachette.co.uk

ACKNOWLEDGEMENTS

A book is the collaboration of a multitude of talented and enthusiastic people, who work together to bring to life what was once an idea. Bringing this book into the world has been a completely joyful process, the fruit of many years of study, trial and error, plus exploration with students, family and friends, to find out what makes each of us thrive and determine how I can condense that into a book of delicious food. Little did Hugh Fearnley-Whittingstall realise when he first floated the idea of running a gut health course at River Cottage, that I was chafing at the bit to share my enthusiasm with a wider audience. Running the course gave me the confidence to put my thoughts on paper. Thank you to everyone who has eaten my food and given me feedback, and to everyone I have taught over the years, especially those on my gut health and fermenting courses – you have also taught me so much.

I am always grateful for good advice and I must thank Antony Topping for his wisdom as I was navigating the uncertain waters of a potential second book. As soon as my brilliant agent, Tim Bates, introduced me to Muna Reyal at Headline, I knew she understood me and my work, and her warmth and steady guidance have been invaluable, reminding me to stay true to that initial desire to write a book for everyone that draws you in because the recipes are great and just happen to improve your gut. Kate Miles at Headline has also been a delightful support throughout the process, offering just the right balance of efficient and silly that makes work seem like play. Anne Sheasby did such a sensitive and seamless job with the copy editing that at times I couldn't believe I hadn't written it that way in the first place!

It was a complete joy that I was able to work with an incredibly talented bunch for the photo shoots: Aya Nishimura (food styling and salad wizardry), Laura Edwards (photography and street lingo), Tabitha Hawkins (prop styling and zumba) and Kendal Noctor (beard modelling and coffee making) – hereafter known as the A-team. The A-team's newest members are Miranda Harvey (whose elegant design talent belies a terrier-like ability to get the best out of the A-team), and Indiana Petrucci, who will now be managing my pronunciation of foreign dishes. To say that the shoots were fun is such an understatement; they were snort-inducingly funny, full of unexpected delight and the sort of company that you wish you could bottle for those grey days.

Ana Zaja Petrak's playfully colourful illustrations perfectly capture the delight I feel for food. I didn't know exactly what I wanted until she drew it, then I fell head over heels in love with it all and now I can't imagine the book any other way.

Thank you also to Radiya Hafiza and Sarah Badhan, who beavered away behind the scenes, and to Georgina Moore and Phoebe Swinburn, who have made it their mission to get the book out there in the world in such a charming way.

I must also express my gratitude to the people whose work I have read and absorbed in my quest for knowledge. My fermenting heroes: Sandor Ellix Katz, Kirsten and Christopher Shockey, Penny Porteous and Olia Hercules. My nutrition heroes: Mark Sisson, Chris Kresser, Tim Spector and Mark Hyman. My food heroes: Giorgio Locatelli, Diana Henry, Jane Grigson, Sam and Sam Clark, Mark Diacono, Rachel Roddy, Tom Hunt, Gill Meller, Ian Pennington, Matthew Pennington, Jack Bevan, Cass Titcombe, Radhika Mohandas and Jollyon Carter. My gut heroes: Jeff Leach, Rob Knight, Paul O'Toole, Martin Blaser, David Perlmutter and Giulia Enders. Thank you all for the guidance and inspiration you have given me over the years.

Finally, to Nick and Finn Devlin, my much loved erstwhile tasters, washer uppers and steadfast supporters during the high intensity process of writing a book; thank you for keeping me sane and grounded – I couldn't have done it without you.